Visitor's G
RHODI

## About the Authors

Brian & Eileen Anderson relished the idea of early retirement to pursue their lifelong interests in travel, flowers, photography and history. Brian read botany 2 years full time at Manchester University before they launched into a new career as travel writers. They have spent a number of years living and travelling around the Mediterranean including around 2 years living in various parts of Greece. When at home, they lecture up and down the country on travel and wild flowers. Brian & Eileen Anderson are also the authors of *Visitor's Guide: Greece* and *Visitor's Guide: Athens and the Peloponnese*.

## Acknowledgement

Special thanks to the Greek National Tourist Office in London who were generous in their support and to Katie Koutroumbakis of the Rhodes Town Tourist Office who answered our many questions with great patience. We would like to express our appreciation to George Barboutis of the Rodos Palace Hotel, Nikos Dimitroulis of Hotel Rodos Princess, George Krisiotis at Hotel Blue Bay (Karpathos) and Hotel Aliki on Symi. To the highly respected *Rodos News* we would like to also say thanks but we save our final cheers for Janet and Uwe for their spiritual support of a more liquid nature and for Mr Max and Moritz for joining us for breakfast every day.

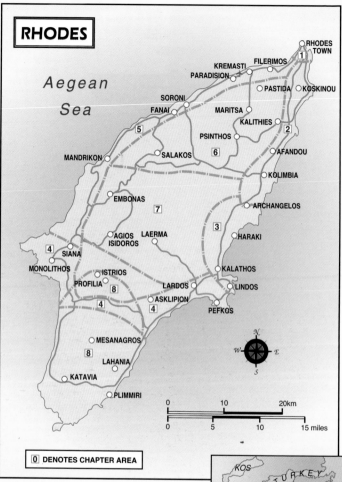

# RHODES

*Aegean*

*Sea*

RHODES TOWN
1
FILERIMOS
KREMASTI
PARADISION
PASTIDA   KOSKINOU
SORONI
FANAI
MARITSA
KALITHIES
2
PSINTHOS
5
AFANDOU
MANDRIKON
SALAKOS
6
KOLIMBIA
EMBONAS
7
ARCHANGELOS
3
LAERMA
AGIOS
ISIDOROS
HARAKI
4
SIANA
MONOLITHOS
ISTRIOS
KALATHOS
PROFILIA
8
LARDOS
LINDOS
ASKLIPION
4
PEFKOS
4
MESANAGROS
8
LAHANIA
KATAVIA
PLIMMIRI

N
W    E
S

| 0 | 10 | 20km |
| 0 | 5 | 10 | 15 miles |

0  DENOTES CHAPTER AREA

KOS
TURKEY
NISSIROS
SYMI
TILOS
HALKI
RHODES
SARIA
KARPATHOS
KASSOS

| 0 | 20 | 40 | 60km |
| 0 | 10 | 20 | 30 miles |

# VISITOR'S GUIDE
# RHODES

Brian & Eileen Anderson

MPC
HUNTER

Published by:
Moorland Publishing Co Ltd,
Moor Farm Road West, Ashbourne,
Derbyshire DE6 1HD England

Published in the USA by:
Hunter Publishing Inc,
300 Raritan Center Parkway, CN 94, Edison, NJ 08818

ISBN 0 86190 556 3

British Library Cataloguing in Publication Data:
A catalogue record for this book is available from the British Library.

Colour origination by: DP Graphics, Wiltshire

Printed in Hong Kong by: Wing King Tong Co Ltd

Cover photograph: St Georges, Lindos (*B. & E. Anderson*)
Rear cover: Pefkos (*B. & E. Anderson*)
Page 3: Prasonissi (*B. & E. Anderson*)

The illustrations have been supplied by Lindsey Porter pp35, 82 top, 182,
183, remainder by Brian & Eileen Anderson

MPC Production Team:
*Editorial*: Tonya Monk
*Editorial Assistant:* Christine Haines
*Design*: Ashley Emery
*Cartography*: Mark Titterton

# CONTENTS

# KEY TO SYMBOLS USED IN TEXT MARGIN AND ON MAPS

| | | | |
|---|---|---|---|
| 🚶 | Recommended walks | ⛪ | Church/Ecclesiastical site |
| 🐟 | Aquatic interest | 🏛 | Building of interest |
| 🏰 | Castle/Fortification | ⊤ | Archaeological site |
| ✳ | Other place of interest | 🏛 | Museum/Art Gallery |
| 🏖 | Beach | 🏔 | Beautiful view/Scenery, Natural phenomenon |
| ⛵ | Water sports | 🕌 | Mosque |
| ⛳ | Golf Club | ✈ | Airport |

## KEY TO MAPS

| | | | |
|---|---|---|---|
| —————— | Main Routes (Surfaced) | ▰ | City/Town |
| —————— | Surfaced Road | ◯ | Town/Village |
| —————— | Stabilised Track | ⌒ | River |
| —————— | Rough Track (4 Wheel Drive) | | |
| - - - - - - - | Ferry Link | | |

## HOW TO USE THIS GUIDE

This MPC Visitor's Guide has been designed to be as easy to use as possible. Each chapter covers a region or itinerary in a natural progression which gives all the background information to help you enjoy your visit. MPC's distinctive margin symbols, the important places printed in bold and a comprehensive index enable the reader to find the most interesting places to visit with ease.

At the end of each chapter an Additional Information section gives specific details such as addresses and opening times, making this guide a complete sightseeing companion.

At the back of the guide the Fact File, arranged in alphabetical order, gives practical information and useful tips to help you plan your holiday before you go and while you are there.

The maps of each region show the main towns, villages, roads and places of interest, but are not designed as route maps and motorists should always use a good recommended road atlas.

# Introduction

Beyond the glittering array of tall, slender masts of luxurious yachts in Mandraki harbour lie the sturdy medieval walls of Rhodes old town. No mere relic of the past, the old town houses a thriving community which bustles with activity, tourist shops, tavernas, bars, houses and even hotels. This is the heartbeat of Rhodes town in the eyes of the tourist, but the commercial heart beats in the modern city lying outside the old town walls. Ancient and modern, this is Rhodes, an island which borrows incessantly from the passing of time while relinquishing nothing. An island where harmony reigns between the old and the new, where a sophisticated north rubs shoulders with a rural south.

Its shoreline is its playground enjoyed by the Greeks and visitors alike. Sandy beaches, shingle beaches, large beaches, small beaches, busy beaches, quiet beaches, Rhodes has them all. Water sports in variety with activities to meet every need but if its just a restful sunbed in the shadow of a giant umbrella in striking distance of a bar, it will not be difficult to find. When the cultural appetite grows there is plenty of sustenance around; three ancient cities await, Lindos, Kamiros and Ialysos, medieval castles in Rhodes town and Monolithos, and countryside excursions to the Valley of the Butterflies, to the seven springs, Efta Pigis or to the top of the second highest mountain on the island, Profitis Ilias.

The following chapters are presented as tours, not just through the landscape but through history, culture and sometimes the natural history, to reveal the facets of Rhodes which drew hordes of invaders in the past and still does in the guise of tourism. The first chapter takes Rhodes Town by storm while the next four leisurely tour adjacent sections around the perimeter of the island which, taken together, offer a complete round-the-island tour. Inland Rhodes is not forgotten with three chapters devoted to all the small inland villages where an old lifestyle is still to be found. For those intent on trying an offshore excursion, the final chapter is there to enrich the experience.

## Rhodes by Name: Sunshine or Roses by Nature?

There are plenty of theories on how Rhodes, or Rodos in Greek, earned its name but no great certainty. One of the least attractive relates to snakes. In antiquity the island was infested with them so the name may have derived from an old Phoenician word, *jarod* or *erod*, meaning snake. According to legend, it was to eradicate snakes that the ancients introduced deer. On a more appealing theme, Rodos may have been born from the Greek word *rodon* meaning rose (*triandafyllo* is now more commonly used). It would be convincing if Rhodes was renowned for its roses in antiquity but it is not especially, except for rock roses which are abundant on the island. Also common on the island are *roidon*, or pomegranate, and this is a strongly favoured contender by some.

The Greeks might have invented logic but they are romantics at heart and have always been quick to cast it aside for a good myth. Forget all the theories and just look back into deep history. Zeus overlooked the sun god Helios when assigning islands. Fortunately, a new island rose from the sea which solved the problem. This was given Helios who then took up residence with his intended, Rodos, named the island after her and gifted it with perpetual sunshine.

Just to add to the confusion, archaeologists have turned up some old Rhodian coins with the head of the sun god Helios on one side and a flower, thought to be a pomegranate, on the other.

*preceding page; The ruined medieval castle of the Knights of St John, Halki*

# People and Culture

In spite of the island's turbulent history and the parade of masters over the centuries, the people of Rhodes have never lost their Greekness. Their conviviality and hospitality to strangers wins the island many friends. Sadly, these qualities are subdued by the pressure of work in the height of the tourist season but never squashed. Away from all the bustle, it takes only a cheerful greeting, sometimes only a smile, to be on the receiving end of their hospitality. It may take the form of an orange pulled from a bag or a handful of freshly grown broad beans but whatever it is, it is considered bad manners to refuse. Language barriers do not exist for the Greeks and mostly they will chatter away in their native tongue in the full expectancy that you will understand some or part of whatever they are saying. Body language and gesticulations play a full part too. The head is frequently used this way. Assent is signified by a slight nod to the side and no is indicted by a slight toss of the head upward often accompanied by a slight 'tchh' sound. If words fail, an invitation to come or to follow is mostly by a downward pawing movement of the hand. If this is an invitation into the home, the first offering will be some sweet preserves served with a glass of water. To refuse this is to refuse their hospitality but it is not essential to eat all of it. No matter how poor the hosts, any suggestion of payment will cause deep offence but a small present for a child would be acceptable. The surprise arrival of a bottle of wine or ouzo on your table in the taverna may well be the gift of a new acquaintance. The custom here is to pour a glass to toast the sender and drink at least a little of the bottle but there will be no expectation that it is all consumed. The penetration of polite conversation often takes visitors by surprise. After the usual health enquiries, which are taken seriously by the Greeks, the conversation quickly moves into questions about the family, how many sons, daughters and their ages. Unreserved admiration is expressed for parents of large families especially with many sons. From this point enquiries continue about work and will invariably contain a question which throws unprepared visitors almost into a state of shock; 'How much do you earn?' In Greek society it would be considered impolite not to ask.

The family unit is strong and still the basis of Greek society, although there are signs that the bonds are starting to weaken under western influences. It is sons who receive the adulation and are totally spoilt by their parents. This does not mean that daughters are not welcomed, as in some societies, and the ideal family is regarded as one son and one daughter. It is remarkable just how many Greek families comprise just two children. In reality they have been using abortion as a means of birth control for a long time. Parental influence is still strong when the time is right for their children to marry. Arranged marriages have not entirely disappeared but they are no longer the norm but

The splendour of medieval Rhodes Town provides inspiration for artists

parents still have a dominant role in satisfying the demands of society and tradition. It is the duty of the son to stand by his parents to ensure that suitable matches are made for all his sisters before he can contemplate marriage. Although a dowry is no longer a legal requirement, and this repeal was only in recent times, it is still perpetuated. A girl goes into marriage often with the gift of a furnished house or apartment from her parents. It remains the girls property and her security. In the same way gifts of gold to the bride, also to provide for her security, are not unusual. At least the newly wedded couple start life without the burden of debt and are able to build and plan a future for their own children. The family unit extends into business too. The Greek preference is for self employment, failing that a secure job with the state, and most of the small businesses employ only family which are eventually passed down via sons and daughters.

It is a male dominated society in which it is demeaning for a man to indulge in women's tasks. This distinct role division is ingrained into society and a woman would lose face if her man was seen sweeping floors or washing dishes. Attitudes are slowly changing amongst the younger generation. The segregation of the sexes too is inbuilt into society. When family or friends enjoy a meal in a taverna, which can be quite a boisterous affair, there is usually a polarisation where the men cluster to one end of the table and the women to the other. Only men have the freedom to go out alone and it is not uncommon to see them dining out in groups but the young mostly head for the bars and congregate there in large numbers. Again signs of change are evident even in this area and young women are becoming part of the social scene. The role of women in the broader society has been recognised in legislation. They acquired the vote only in 1952 and the first woman Deputy was elected to Parliament the following year. Sexual discrimination in career opportunities and in the place of work has been outlawed. Many practical steps have been taken to assist the integration of women as equals in society. Low cost nurseries providing child places have been provided to free women to work and they have acquired rights of ownership after marriage and an equal share of communal property on divorce. Women now hold important posts in all branches of the Civil Service and in commerce but, in spite of all their progress, equality is only accepted in the big cities. Throughout rural Greece it remains contrary to the culture and fundamental change will only be fully accepted very slowly. For women travelling alone in Greece there are no exceptional problems. The incidence of violent crime, including rape, is much lower than in other western societies. But it is not unknown and the same wariness of the possible situations should be observed. Greek men firmly believe that they are irresistible to all women so their attentions can be expected. Rhodes is very cosmopolitan and women alone in bars or tavernas are an accepted part of the scenery.

# Geography and Topography

Rhodes is the largest island of the Dodecanese group which lies in the south-east Aegean Sea scrambled around the coast of Asia Minor. Dodecanese translates to twelve islands but there are normally fourteen assigned to this group as well as some forty uninhabited islets. In shape Rhodes resembles an almond with the symmetry spoilt only by opposing headlands. Its 52 mile (84km) length lies on a north-east south-west axis with the northern end approaching to within 7 miles (11km) of the Turkish coastline while the widest distance, 22 miles (35km), is measured between Cape Mitias in the east and Cape Armenistos in the west.

Along with Crete and Karpathos, Rhodes is regarded as part of the 'Cretan arc', the land which once linked the Peloponnese with Asia Minor. Tectonic plate movements and upheavals in Tertiary times left only the summits of a mountain chain visible above sea level, which are now these islands. The arc forms the southern boundary of the Aegean and separates it from the Mediterranean. Thus the west coast of Rhodes borders the Aegean sea while the east coast bathes in the Mediterranean.

Much of the central part of the island is hilly but there are only two regions of significantly high ground. Mount Ataviros, a large, barren mass of grey rock overlooking the village of Embonas, is the highest standing at an elevation of 4,000ft (1,215m). Its steep slopes make it look inaccessible but ascent on foot is easily accomplished by experienced walkers. The other region, Mount Profitis Ilias, lies north of this and, at 2,960ft (900m), is appreciably lower and well covered by vegetation. The central upland area gathers abundant winter rainfall and is well furnished with rivers and streams. Many of these rage in winter, especially after storms, and cut out wide beds at the lower levels but few are perennial.

Land suitable for cultivation is scattered in pockets around the island, some of it reclaimed from the hillsides by the use of terracing. None of the areas, except perhaps those in the south-east, are large enough to be intensively farmed by modern methods and equipment.

# Politics

Politics are an overriding obsession with the Greeks. Free political expression arrived only in 1974 with the fall of the dictatorship. All the 300 seats in the single chamber parliament are filled by parties formed after 1974. Essentially a two party system is evolving with the contestants being the socialist PASOK, the Panhellenic Socialist Movement and the New Democracy party (ND) with conservative leanings. Not without some support is the Communist Party of Greece, the KKE. All these symbols are liberally painted on bridges and buildings throughout the country. After years of socialist rule, the New Democracy under Mitsotakis held the balance of power by the slenderest of margins, one seat, for a time but the elections of 1993 saw the control swing back to PASOK led by the ageing Papandreou. The political system is slowly maturing but it still faces some serious problems in bureaucracy, nepotism, petty corruption, low productivity and poor social services. Greece's membership of the EEC has itself been a stabilising influence and the country has benefited greatly from grants, enormous loans and subsidies over recent years. A stabilisation programme imposed from Brussels is currently in place trying to reduce government spending and bring inflation under control. Regardless of which party holds the balance of power, strikes are a way of life in Greece and barely a week passes without some sector providing the action. It does occasionally become a serious problem for the traveller when the action moves into a concerted phase and banks, transport and tavernas, for example, all co-ordinate their strikes.

For the Greeks, politics is a passion akin to football and demands the same loyalty. The uncommitted or floating voter is a rare species. Prime time Saturday evening television is often filled with 2 hours of political debate which is avidly followed even in the tavernas. Visitors may not escape being drawn into political discussion and are likely to be tested on three main topics; relations between Greece and Turkey, the Cyprus question and, a more recent concern, Macedonia.

## Economy

Tourism now plays a leading role and over the past decade it has given a considerable boost to the building industry with the demand for hotels, apartments, restaurants and bars, to road construction and to the service sector in general. Tourism is easily the major earner of hard currency.

Outside tourism, agriculture still remains important and touches many of the islanders even though they may have other employment. This is largely a consequence of the dowry and inheritance laws which sees the land constantly divided into small parcels. Land sales or bartering within a family will sometimes coalesce adjoining plots but customs in general keep the plots well divided and ensures that virtually every Rhodian has land to farm. It also makes the application of modern farming methods with big machinery impractical. Grain, especially wheat, is a major crop but quick maturing barley is grown in winter as a feed crop and red oats in summer.

Fruits are important too and there is none more important than the olive. Citrus fruits are also popular and extensive orange groves are seen around Massari and Malona. It is along the main road here that orange vendors pitch their stalls through the early part of the season to catch the passing trade. The vine too is extensively grown for the island's wine and the favoured locations are on the cooler side of the island around Embonas. Two other specialities of Rhodes are melons and water melons which can be seen growing in the fields down in the south of the island, especially around Apolakia.

Fishing remains a small but important sector and tourism has helped to sustain it. The fleet is nothing more than an armada of small boats based in the coastal villages around the island. Even Faliraki, a major tourist resort, still has a small bay where fishing boats anchor.

Cottage industries, especially pottery, have flourished under tourism. Keramik factories litter the highways always with large car parks to accommodate coaches and most tourist shops sell some pottery. Hand made carpets, a feature of the island just a decade ago, have declined in importance but are still to be seen in the shops.

## Law and Order

The incidence of violent crime, rape, theft and robbery is still far lower than in most other western cultures but not absent. Although sensible precautions are always advisable, it is not something that need concern the tourist too much. It still pays to be sensible with personal property, especially cameras, and protect it as at home. It is said that most of the petty thievery arrives and leaves with the visitors but with plenty of Albanians around now, they too are shouldering some of the blame. Generally, the Greeks have their own moral code for living in which there are some distinctly eastern traits and ambiguities. They have a basic honesty which means that if you leave your change in their shop then they will chase down the street after you to return it. On the other hand, the same owner may well have twisted you out of a few *drachmas* by quoting a wrong price. This is regarded as smart and foreigners are fair game. Their attitude to the laws in general are not always easy to comprehend. There are many laws which the public just totally and completely ignore. Parking is one of them. It is hard to find a parking space even where a street is littered with no parking signs. Periodically the police come along with parking tickets but so few ever get paid for various reasons so the parking continues. It is the same with safety belts in cars. The law is very explicit on this, safety belts are compulsory but drivers rarely wear them. Every few months there is an announcement that the fine is to be increased for this offence and that there will be a check in a few days time. On the day of the check seat belts are worn and on the following day everything reverts to as it was. There is also a law that motorcyclists should wear crash helmets but motorcyclists do not wear them and bikes for hire are offered without crash helmets. Disobedience of these driving laws is visible, it can be observed every day of the week but the same philosophy applies to many laws in every day life.

# Religion

The Orthodox Church is firmly established and dominates the religious scene. Other denominations are tolerated but proselytisation is not. The Church of Rhodes and the Dodecanese is an autonomous institution and is not controlled by the church of the Greek mainland but owes its allegiance directly to the Ecumenical Patriarch of Constantinople. Head of the church is Metropolitan Bishop of Rhodes and included within the diocese are the islands of Halki, Simi, Tilos and Nisyros.

Priests move about the community in their black ankle-length cassocks, black hat and full beard. They may be seen drinking coffee in the kafenion and travelling by bus when, more than likely, someone will spring up to offer a seat but they are rigidly church based without the role of social worker in the wider community. As in many other western cultures, the church is slowly losing its power amongst the people, especially the younger generation. The acceptance of civil marriage was forced on the church by the government following reforms in 1981. Up until that time, Greeks married abroad by civil ceremony were not accepted as married under the Government's own civil law. Abortion too was legalised, also against church opposition, but this did nothing more than legalise the existing high rate of abortion. It has long been used as a means of family planning and remains, even now, the most widely practised form. The Church still controls a lot of agricultural land and unused land which the government is trying to wrestle away to put into the hands of farmers and co-operatives.

On high days and holy days, and there are many in the Greek calendar, the church comes into its own and, for a brief time becomes the focus of community life. Easter is the most important event of the year and this and other religious events are discussed in the Fact File. The church played an important role throughout the Byzantine years as guardian of the Greek culture. It organised secret schools to educate the children and preserve the language.

# Folk Art

Folk art on Rhodes is very distinctive. Pottery, textiles, woodwork and other expressions of folk art tend to be very traditional and conservative in design. Designs and techniques are handed down from generation to generation with little change or evolution. As in any poor society, the object must also fulfil a function even though it may be decoratively coloured or crafted. Decorative pottery is made throughout the island and is characterised by its vivid coloration with reds, greens and blues. Plates on Rhodes had a special place in the traditional home for decoration and as a display of wealth. Work aimed specifically for the tourist market relies heavily on designs from early history or from Greek mythology. Woven and embroidered textiles are also commonly found throughout the island. Embroidery has proved popular with visitors and it is not uncommon for village ladies to arrange displays along the roadside of tourist trails, especially at Lindos. Museums of folk art are becoming increasingly popular. Outside Rhodes town, there is one at Asklipion and another at Kritinia which are interesting for their displays of national costumes.

## Food and Drink

Eating out in Greece, traditionally inexpensive, is a national pastime but even that is under threat with rising prices and high rates of inflation. It was unthinkable for a Greek family to entertain friends or family to a meal at home. As a party they would head for the taverna and the host would collect the bill. Not only was the taverna a place to eat but it was also a place of entertainment. After the meal, tables would be pushed back, the owner would produce a bouzouki or similar instrument and the menfolk would rise to dance. Perhaps later the women might join the dancing too. Sadly this now happens only on festive occasions. Gone is the bouzouki to be replaced by the television and the atmosphere of the taverna is generally more subdued. Watching the Greeks eat is a pleasure in itself. Seldom do they order individually, instead they order a vast number of communal dishes which fill the table to overflowing. There is no rush to eat the food either, conversation continues at a high pitch while the diners pick and nibble their way steadily through the dishes. They are far less concerned about cold food and many dishes which arrive hot are cold before they are eaten. Some tourists find it a bit disconcerting when their meals are actually served on the cool side but, in most tourist areas, the message that tourists generally like their food hot has registered.

Although the Greek cuisine is quite extensive, tavernas tend only to have a limited menu. Lunch time, between 2 and 3pm after work finishes, is the only meal of the day for which the chef will prepare a range of cooked dishes. For the evening trade, and the Greeks are notoriously late eaters, the menu offers whatever is left over from lunch, which has often been kept warm for hours, and a range of grills which are cooked to order. Charcoal is generally used for grilling and it is not unusual to see large charcoal grills by the doorway or outside in summer. Although the tavernas are the traditional eating places, Rhodes town has a selection of restaurants which provide a better standard of decor in particular and offer a more international cuisine.

Tavernas are obliged to have a menu but many still do not. Instead diners will be shown a glass show case exhibiting the range of dishes available or, and this is still very common in the villages, they will be

## Fast Food Greek Style

The Greeks are great nibblers, particularly in the mornings, so there is no shortage of fast-food. 'Pies' with various fillings, usually made with filo pastry and looking like a Cornish pasty:-

### Savouries

*Tiropitta:* cheese.
*Spanakopitta:* spinach only or with cheese and eggs.
*Kreatopitta:* minced meat.

*Souvlaki:* small pieces of meat on a wooden skewer served with a lump of bread or with pitta.

*Doner me pitta:* slices of meat from the *gyros* (meat cooked on a vertical spit) placed in a pitta parcel with a little yoghurt, tomato and onion.

*Tost:* usually a slice of ham and cheese toasted between bread.

*Koulouria:* Sesame seed encrusted rings are available from bread shops.

Freshly pressed orange juice is widely available.

### Sweets

*Milopitta:* apple.
*Bougatza:* vanilla custard

led into the kitchen to see exactly what is cooking. If difficulties are experienced in the final choice then spoons may appear for a tasting session. In an effort to improve standards, there has been a recent government decree instructing that all tables should have a cloth table cloth. Previously it was usual just to have a plain piece of polythene which was changed for each new client. It served a double purpose because at the end of the meal all scraps from the plates would be tipped into it and the whole lot bundled up and removed. Now the situation has changed. Tables are fitted with a decorative table cloth but this is securely protected by a polythene sheet covered by paper square and only the latter is laid fresh each time. Should there be a menu on the table then it will probably be in Greek and English but it will only show a partial correspondence with the dishes on offer so it still pays to ask. It is unusual to find the table laid, apart from the oil and vinegar flasks, paper napkins and the inevitable toothpicks, but the cutlery arrives with bread after an order is placed.

There is no special form in a taverna and no conventions to follow. The Greeks often go in for a plate of chips and a beer and make it last half the night. For diners though, it is usual to begin with one or a selection of the starters or *mezedes* on offer. These include *tzatsiki* (a yoghurt, cucumber and garlic dip), *taramasalata* (fish roe mixed with potato, oil and vinegar, the pinker the better), *melitzano salata* (an aubergine dip with tomato and garlic) and *humus*, another dip this time from chick-peas. Fresh vegetables are rarely available but two vegetables which turn up as *mezedes* are *gigantes* (butter beans cooked in tomato and oil) and peas (*arakas*). *Saganaki*, fried cheese, is another interesting starter. The waiter will raise an eyebrow if *mezedes* are ordered separately by each individual, even tourists are expected to order a selection and share in Greek style. Salads may be preferred as starters or as part of the starters and the most popular is the village salad or *horiatiki salata* which normally includes lettuce, or cabbage, tomato, onion, cucumber, a certain weight of feta cheese and olives. A few years ago, a salad like this constituted a meal in itself and many tourists were perfectly happy to make a lunch from it. Unfortunately, this made the taverna owner less than happy, consequently the price has risen considerably and they are not always the generous portions they were. Tomatoes, cucumber, feta cheese and lettuce (*maruli*) are all offered as separate dishes. Ready cooked dishes may include the familiar *moussaka*, a mince dish with aubergines, potato and bechamel sauce, veal in tomato, *stifado* (veal stew with onions) or *giovetsi* (oven cooked lamb served with pasta). Chicken cooked on the spit is popular and inexpensive but favoured amongst the grills is *souvlaki*, veal or pork on a skewer. Chops, pork, lamb or veal, are ever present on the evening menus as are *keftedes* (spicy meat balls) and *biftekia* (mince burgers). Fish is sometimes on offer but for a selection it is better to find a fish taverna (*psaria*). Lobster (*astakos*) and red mullet (*barbounia*) are usually top of the menu and are expensive as are shrimps (*garides*). Octopus, grilled or cooked in wine is less expensive as is squid (*kalamari*). At the cheap end is the small whitebait (*marides*) which is eaten in its entirety, head and all. This dish is often available as a starter in a fish restaurant. Desserts are very limited, usually fruit, but the popularity of yoghurt and honey amongst the tourists is now recognised. If you have tucked into your meal with obvious enjoyment, the proprietor may produce a plate of fruit, peeled and presented with his compliments.

Some Greeks prefer to drink ouzo with meals and this is served in small bottles and usually taken with water. Others choose *retsina*, a resinated wine, which is an acquired taste although the local *retsina* on Rhodes is very good. There is a wide selection of wines made on the island and these are featured on page 19.

Apart from Rhodian wines, it is possible that the wine list may contain some of the countries acknowledged good wines like *Boutari Naoussa* and *Lac des Roches* as well as some medium priced popular ones like *Kambas* and *Rotonda*.

# Wine and Dine with Romance

In spite of the fact that Rhodes attracts mass tourism, there are still a good number of places to dine on the island where the atmosphere is charged with romance. Maybe it is just a good ambience in a small bay with the table set on the edge of the sea or amongst natural surroundings or in such isolation it feels like a different world. Although this is by no means an exhaustive list, below are ten suggestions for different parts of the island. Almost all these have been mentioned in the appropriate chapter. Some of the more isolated tavernas may not be open in the evening.

**Traganou:** at the extreme northern end of Afandou beach, this small taverna is most easily found by taking the road opposite the most southerly Kalithies road. There is an uninterrupted view from the veranda to the milky blue sea.

**Kolimbia beach:** a long avenue of mature eucalyptus trees makes for a romantic entrance down to Cape Vagia; turn right at the bottom then ahead at cross-roads for the taverna in the small bay.

**Epta Pigis:** set beneath the trees and by the trickling streams, it is a place with plenty of rustic atmosphere and life. On top of all that, the Greek food is good.

**Haraki:** this intimate bay is a delightful place to dine on a warm summer's evening. Stefanos taverna is right on the sea front, small and with only outside tables. For something a little more upmarket, try Argos restaurant on the headland.

**Gennadion:** a rising star in the tourism stakes, its beach tavernas still have peaceful locations. Try the menu in Memories restaurant.

**Kiotari:** on the coast south of Lindos, turn left opposite the Asklipion road. The Lighthouse restaurant along the track to the right at the sea front has a good position on a quiet and scenic beach.

**Plimmiri:** this is down towards the southern tip and the taverna here has one huge sweep of bay all to itself and not a sun umbrella in sight!

**Prasonissi:** this is virtually island's end. The tavernas are located right on the beach but the script on the wall, pray for wind, is for the benefit of the windsurfers and has nothing to do with the food!

**Glyfada Beach:** located 4 miles (6km) down an unsurfaced track, really is away from it all! Two fish tavernas to choose from but Paradise taverna has the best location right on the sea front.

**Akroyiali:** just north of the Ancient Kamiros road, this is superbly located on a quiet stretch of coast. Great for just sitting and drinking in the atmosphere.

# Flora and Fauna

The rich and colourful parade of wild flowers on Rhodes is almost totally reserved for the spring months of March, April and May. The long, hot, dry summer is too stressful for plant growth, it is more a test of survival. But the plants do survive using a whole variety of adaptations. Trees and shrubs have made use of deep tap roots to get down nearer the water or devices to minimise water lost by transpiration. Strategies to save water include thick bark, narrow, rolled leaves with minimum surface area, a thick, leathery leaf cuticle, a covering of dense hair, often thick and felty, or special glands to release oil onto the outer surfaces. All these strategies can be seen on Rhodes, not just seen but smelt. It is the oily plants which fill the summer air with that heady, herby aromatic aroma.

For the other plants, it is time to retire for a period of resting. With the annuals, this is easy. All they do is ripen and disperse seed and die, confident that the autumn rains will awake and nourish the next generation. Others, the geophytes, retire to a resting bud below ground and await the passing of summer. These are mostly the plants with below ground storage organs, bulbs, rhizomes or tubers, and there are many of these on Rhodes as there are throughout the Mediterranean where a similar climate persists.

The growth season starts in autumn with the first rains, usually late October. In many ways, this corresponds to early spring in Europe. There is an instant flush of flowers, like *Cyclamen graecum, Scilla autumnalis, Sternbergia lutea* and a number of *Colchicum* species. All these leap from the earth straight into flower without the formality of growing leaves, they follow sometime later. Mainly, it is time for steady growth and the dry brown landscape is transformed rapidly into a sea of green as the grass and herbs get underway. Now too is the lambing season if the lush new grass is not to be missed, although it is kids that are more likely to be seen on Rhodes. January begins the next season of flowers, anemones and muscari start to add their colour. February adds still more species to the list but the main display is saved for March and April. By May the greenness of the landscapes has lost all its brightness and brown tones steadily assume command. Lowland flowers diminish rapidly and only in a cool, wet season are there many to be seen by the end of the month. Events are later in the mountains where the floral display is extended for a further week or two.

Significant forests still exist on Rhodes, not as they were 3,000 years ago before man's interference, but there are extensive areas of *Pinus brutia* and *Cupressus sempervirens*. Unfortunately, fire is a natural hazard especially with all the aromatic, highly volatile and highly inflammable oils produced by the plants themselves. It takes so little to start a fire in the forest and the greatest care and vigilance is required by all visitors in summer. Rhodes experienced one of their worst fires in recent history back in 1987. Left to its own devices, burnt areas usually respond with new growth very quickly. A lot of the shrubs in particular are quite resistant and will sprout into growth the next season. Seeds which have lain dormant for perhaps years have a new opportunity and for the following few years there is a great abundance of annuals, biennials and bulb forming plants. The trees restart themselves by seed but take many years to reach maturity. Grazing animals are one of the biggest dangers to the regeneration process. If they are allowed to feed freely on the abundance of new growth and the regeneration checked, the whole process takes a different course. Soil erosion becomes a major factor and, with the loss of humus and water holding capacity, subsequent regrowth is severely hampered.

There are two particular plant communities which the visitor is most likely to notice travelling around the island. The *macchie*, the fairly tall shrub community, usually around shoulder height or more, and the *phrygana* made up of dwarf, knee high shrubs often rounded or domed. There is a fair mixture of species in both communities. In the drier areas, the *macchie* is characterised by shrubs or small trees such as the kermes or holly oak, *Quercus coccifera*, the eastern strawberry tree, *Arbutus andrachne*, the strawberry tree, *A. unedo*, *Erica manipulifera* and *Calicotome villosa*. In damp valley bottoms the myrtle, *Myrtus communis*, *Styrax officinalis* may also be present. Generally, the macchie allows little to develop beneath so the ground flora is poor or absent. *Phrygana* is particularly well developed on Rhodes and is generally much more interesting. Two shrubs in particular often dominate, these are *Euphorbia acanthothamnos* and *Sarcopoterium spinosum.* Both are domed, spiny and look as though they are made from wire netting. Their open structure sometimes provides a refuge for wild orchids and, where grazing is heavy, it might be the only place they can survive. There are plenty of other species too making up the *phrygana* including the rock roses which are common on the island. The *phrygana* is open enough to allow a ground flora to develop and is often a good place to look for flowers in the spring, especially annuals and wild orchids.

The fields of red poppies, the yellow and white chrysants and the white anthemis daisies all attract attention but there are some flowers which cause the visitor more excitement than others. One of the stars is the lovely white *Paeonia clusii ssp rhodia* which can be found at a number of locations but chiefly on Mount Profitis Ilias. There are three species of cyclamen on the island too, *C. graecum*, which flowers in the autumn and the spring flowering *C. persicum* and the much more common *C. repandum*. There is just one fritillary to find *Fritillaria rhodia* which grows at a number of stations around the island and one tulip, *Tulipa saxatilis* but this is hard to find. Less difficult to find, but still not easy, are the two narcissus, *N. serotinus* and *N. tazetta* but the jewels in the crown are the wild orchids which are widespread around the island. These are featured on pages 144 and 145.

*Dracunculus vulgaris*

*Papaver rhoeas*

*Rana arborea*

*Cistus creticus*

*Orchis anatolica*

*Orchis coriophora*

*Campanula hagiela*

*Ophrhs tenthredinifera*

*Paeonia clusii ssp rhodia*

*Orchis papilionaceae*

*Agama stelio*

*Ranunculus asiaticus*

Mediterranean islands are not especially known for their wildlife but Rhodes is better than most. One of the biggest surprises is the presence of deer on the island although the only ones seen were in captivity. They are the symbol of Rhodes and have pride of place at the harbour entrance. Legend relates that they were introduced in antiquity but it is thought they were reintroduced to the island in the Middle Ages by the Knights of St John and subsequently hunted out of existence by the Turks. The Italians reintroduced them early in the twentieth century and they may now have been hunted out of existence yet again.

Petaloudes, or the Valley of the Butterflies, one of the more remarkable wildlife features on the island is used as a major tourist attraction. This cool, moist valley is home to the Jersey tiger moth, *Euplagia quadripunctaria*, and it is here that they gather by the thousands for their summer rest. Spread around the valley, they remain huddled on the trees until the autumn. More details are given in the feature on page 131. Generally, it is a good island for butterflies and there is a wide selection to be seen in flight throughout the summer, with May, June and July perhaps the best months.

In antiquity the island was infested with snakes, less so now but they are still around in the countryside although most are harmless. The farmers no longer find it necessary to wear knee length leather boots to guard against the one small species of viper as they did only a decade ago. Lizards too are everywhere but the one to watch out for is the Rhodes dragon, *Agama stellio*. It occurs on a number of Greek islands but not in such numbers as on Rhodes. It is very large and its size, adults can reach 12 inches (30cm), helps to distinguish it as do the roughly diamond-shaped markings down its back. The colour is variable from light brown to grey with males the more colourful. It likes hot, dry places so keep an eye on stone walls and rocks. Drivers might see it charging across the road at great speed with its head held high. Tree frogs are not uncommon on the island and they are mostly spotted basking in the sun on a tree branch usually close to water.

Hunters still regard birds as a delicacy so their activities keep down the numbers but there is still a good variety of small birds amongst which the bee-eater is common. Its liquid chrrup call, once recognised, is very distinctive. Telephone wires are a favourite perch and, in the south of the island particularly, they are present in large flocks. Common too are the hooded crow and the jay but from the acropolis at Lindos it is possible to see colonies of lesser kestrels while across on the other coast, at Monolithos, the shy blue rock thrushes are around. Also spotted were woodchat shrike and the black-eared wheatear.

# History

The very early disjointed strands of history coalesce into a story with the formation of the three ancient cities, Ialysos, Kamiros and Lindos. Ialysos on the slopes of Mount Filerimos, just west of the northern tip of the island, seems to have been favoured by the early settlers. Archaeological evidence suggests that the Phoenicians had a settlement there and later, around 1500BC, the Minoans had developed a trading post at nearby Trianda. Significant development took place with the arrival of the Mycenaeans from Achaea about a century later. They brought their own culture, including the Greek language, and the custom of building fortified citadels on strategic hilltops, especially where these guarded fertile plains. In this way the three ancient cities were settled and the island became a flourishing Mycenaean centre.

Next came the Dorians around 1100BC. The Dorians were a Greek speaking tribe who swept down from the north into central and southern Greece to overwhelm first the mainland Mycenaeans then later island communities such as on Rhodes. They divided the island into three sectors under the cities of Lindos, Ialysos and Kamiros. The following centuries, the Dark Age, up to around 800BC, are vague from a lack of knowledge and understanding, not just of Rhodes but throughout the whole region. Changes in the structure of society mark the end of this period. The autocratic rule of the Mycenaean age gave way to City-states. These enjoyed a more liberal regime which bore elements of democracy and under which the individual had greater freedom of self-expression, intellectually, politically and artistically. Written records too started in this period which gave this first reliable insight into early history. The works of Homer were written down by 750BC in which Ialysos, Kamiros, and Lindos are all mentioned.

## SEA TRADE

The island's location made it the focal point of a seaways trading network between east and west and north and south. Routes that ran from Sicily to Argolis then via the Cyclades to Rhodes and on to Cyprus and Syria and from the Ionian coast of Asia minor down through Rhodes to Egypt. Rhodes prospered as evidenced by the coins minted on the island as early as the sixth century BC.

These three cities on Rhodes remained politically independent of each but formed a league with other nearby Dorian cities on Kos and in Asia Minor, Halicarnassus and Knidos, known as the Hexapolis, the six cities. This unity balanced the power of the Ionian cities on Asia Minor. Ultimately, the danger came from a different direction, from Persia, and by 490BC Rhodes was coming under attack. By 479BC the island had decided to place itself under the jurisdiction of Athens by joining the Delian Confederacy. It did not last too long for in 411BC, towards the end of the Peloponnesian War, the island switched allegiance to Sparta.

## SYNOECISM

In 408BC, after the break with Athens, the three cities decided to join and found a new trading centre on the northern tip of the island where Rhodes town still stands today. This in turn led to the gradual decline of the original cities. The new city was laid out on a grid system of intersecting streets according to the principles attributed to Hippodamus of Miletus although it is doubtful that Hippodamus himself was directly involved. The town's five harbours were the best equipped in the Aegean which ensured it maintained its strong trading position.

The conquests of Alexander the Great brought even greater trading opportunities for Rhodes in Egypt and Syria so they were quick to side with the Macedonians. Alexander, an admirer of the political system on Rhodes, used it as a model when founding the new city of Alexandria in 331BC. The stability of the island was thrown into turmoil following the death of Alexander. Although Alexander's empire remained unified in the short term, the lack of a royal successor resulted in power passing to the generals in the provinces and it was not long before they were warring between themselves. Antigonus, governor of Syria and Anatolia, took the lead in trying to re-establish unity throughout the empire. Rhodes was strong enough to stand alone and it remained independent. When Antigonus asked Rhodes to join it in battle against Egypt, a major trading partner, it rightly refused. In 305BC, Demetrios the Poliorcet (Besieger), son of Antigonus, launched an attack on Rhodes which is recorded now as one of the most glorious battles in its history.

## THE SIEGE

Backed by an army of 40,000 men well armed with the most sophisticated siege machines of the age, Demetrios confidently expected to overthrow the Rhodians mustering around 25,000 including help from both Crete and Egypt. For a whole year Demetrios tried in vain and even his ultimate weapon, the Helipolis, a nine storey assault tower on wheels of oak, failed to breach the walls, although it did cause considerable damage. After mediation from other Greek cities, Antigonus asked Demetrios to conclude a truce with the Rhodians and withdraw. The treaty guaranteed its independence and upheld the honour of its people. Almost by necessity, Demetrios left behind the dreaded Helipolis and other heavy siege equipment which was sold and the proceeds used to build an offering to the gods. From this the Colossus of Rhodes, the statue of the sun god Helios was built by Chares of Lindos. The Colossus had a relatively short life. It was destroyed by the violent earthquake of 227BC which also destroyed a large part of the city and the shipyards.

## THE PRIME OF RHODES

Rhodes, already a rich and influential city, developed further throughout the Hellenistic period becoming a major centre of learning and of the arts. It came to rival other famous intellectual centres like Alexandria and Pergamum and became one of the main schools of sculpture. Some of the products of Rhodian sculpture, including Aphrodite of Rhodes, are to be seen in the museum in Rhodes old town but most are scattered around and appear in museums throughout the western world. It also attracted painters, poets, and historians but its high reputation was earned mainly by its philosophers and orators. Panaetios, son of Nicagoras, was one of the island's most famous philosophers who eventually became head of the stoic school in Athens.

## RHODES AND THE ROMANS

In the latter part of the Hellenistic period, Rhodes was increasingly drawn to the emerging power in the west, Rome. Rhodes had a good record in managing its political affairs prudently by the simple expedient of keeping its trading interests central and avoiding taking sides. At the end of the third century, as the Romans grew stronger and showed more interference in Greek affairs, Rhodes decided on taking a friendly attitude to the Romans. It gradually accepted Rome's enemies as her own and became involved in war alongside the Romans against Antiochus III of Syria. Here the Rhodian admiral, Eudamos, defeated Hanibal, the great enemy of the Romans and the military advisor to Antiochus in the sea battle of Side (190BC). In the settlement between Antiochus and the Romans which followed, Caria and Lycia were given to Rhodes. Now Rhodes occupied a position of power but it did not last, nor did the gratitude of the Romans. The Lycians agitated constantly for independence and were frequently complaining about Rhodes to the Roman Senate. When the Rhodians showed reluctance to join the Romans in their battle with Perseus (168BC), the Romans retaliated by taking away Caria and Lycia and by declaring Delos in the Cyclades a free port which destroyed Rhodes' trade at a stroke. Cassius inflicted perhaps the final blow to Rhodes when he laid siege to the island in 42BC with devastating effect. This was a reprisal for the island's refusal to join him against his enemies after the death of Julius Caesar. He was relentless in his destruction, killed many of the inhabitants, stripped off many of the treasures and declared he would leave nothing but the sun.

Rhodes like the rest of Greece, slowly withered away into sad decline hastened by the great earthquake of AD155.

## MEDIEVAL RHODES

The history in the early centuries AD after the visit of St Paul and the island's conversion to Christianity is at best fragmentary. It is known that the Goths plundered the island in AD263 just as they had sacked Ephesus in Asia Minor and Heraion on Samos.

When the Roman's divided their empire on a language basis, the Latin speaking west was administered from Rome but the Greek speaking east came under Byzantium. Constantine reunited the empire with leadership from Byzantium which was enlarged to become Constantinople. The empire again divided but this time it became, by AD395, a permanent division. The western part of the empire eventually collapsed under the constant assaults of the barbarian invaders but the Byzantine empire survived in the east until around the eleventh century. It was by no means a settled existence and the Byzantine empire was constantly under threat especially from Persia. Although Rhodes managed to retain its Greek character, the island suffered invasions from time to time, notably by the Persians in the seventh century and later by the Arabs and the Turks. It never managed to rebuild its trade or recover its former prosperity, at least not until the start of the Crusades.

Rhodes became a staging post on the way to the Holy Land and by 1097 Rhodian ships were carrying supplies to the Crusading armies. In 1191 Richard the Lion Heart of England and later Philip of France both docked at Rhodes with their fleets. Venice had established trade with the island perhaps before the Crusades grew in importance and accordingly was granted special privileges by the Byzantine Emperor Alexios Comnenos in 1082. The Venetian's domination of the island lasted only until the Emperor's death. In 1204 when Constantinople was sacked by the Franks, the Byzantine empire was again under threat and the Aegean islands were taken over by various Italian states. Rhodes declared itself independent under the leadership of Leon Gavalas, a wealthy landowner and official of Constantinople. Gavalas was unable to defend the island against hostilities from Venice and an alliance in 1234 returned Rhodes to Byzantium and granted commercial privileges to Venice. There was still no settled existence for throughout the thirteenth century both the Genoese and the Venetians fiercely contested possession of the island. Genoa emerged triumphant when a treaty signed by Emperor Michael Palaeologos gave it trading supremacy. Soon control of the island was to pass to the Knights of St John.

## KNIGHTS OF ST JOHN

The Order of the Knights of St John, like the Templars and the Teutonic Order emerged from the Crusades. Originally the Knights were a religious and charitable order evolving from a hospice dedicated to St John the Baptist founded by Italian merchants in the eleventh century. Their duties related to the care of Christian pilgrims visiting Jerusalem and they were known as Hospitallers. After the first Crusade, the Hospitallers became more actively involved in the wars against the Moslems and emerged with a military order to extend their protective role beyond nursing and care. It evolved into a structured organisation with the knights representing the military wing, the brothers in charge and the nursing care and the clergy for spiritual matters. In 1291, with the eventual failure of the Crusades, the Knights lost their headquarters at Ptolemais in northern Palestine and took refuge in Cyprus. A relatively short time later, in 1306 they bought Rhodes, Kos and Leros from the Genoan admiral Vignolo and 3 years later they were firmly established on Rhodes.

## THE CASTLES

With the need to defend themselves, the Knights indulged in considerable building activity and rebuilt Rhodes town in such a robust style that it stands hardly changed to this present day. The Acropolis at Lindos was converted to a stronghold and other castles were built around the island, notably at Monolithos, Archangelos, Kritinia, Feraklos and Asklipion. Watchtowers were built around the whole coast and kept manned. The chain of defence against the east stretched to other islands and castles were also built on neighbouring islands including Halki, Symi, Tilos, Nisiros, Kos, Kalymnos and Leros.

Under the protection of the Knights, the native Rhodians were generally loyal but had little political power. Their numbers were swelled by immigrant craftsmen mainly from Spain, Italy and France who were skilled in shipbuilding, engineering, architecture and even in banking. With the Jews being expelled from Spain, a large population built up on Rhodes where they settled in the south-east section of the city.

When the fleet sent by Mohammed II the Conqueror besieged the city in 1480, it was successfully defended by the Knights under the Great Magister Pierre d'Aubusson. Later, in 1522, when besieged by an even greater force under Sultan Suleiman II, the Magnificent, the Knights held out for 6 months before finally capitulating and leaving for Malta. Rhodes remained under Turkish rule until 1912.

## TURKISH RULE (1522-1912)

Events of the Turkish rule are not too well recorded but it seems that Rhodes, as a conquered island, was not granted the privileges which Suleiman granted to other islands in the Dodecanese. Instead, a resident governor was installed with a garrison. The Greeks were excluded from the walled city at night and were obliged to develop new settlements outside.

The Turks were content to assume military control and did not involve themselves in trade or commerce to any great extent and left that to the Rhodians. Soon the island was trading freely with Europe and other parts of the empire and prospering reasonably well. Apart from converting Latin churches into mosques, the Turks made no wholesale attempt to convert the Greeks to Islam and the Rhodians were given almost complete cultural autonomy which proved a major factor in preserving the Greek way of life.

During the Greek revolution against the Turks in the early part of the nineteenth century, Rhodes was unable to participate directly although many islanders went to the mainland to fight. Fearing revolution, the Turks imposed a tighter control on the island and its way of life. In 1866, a campaign was launched to force Rhodes and some of the Dodecanese islands into an Ottoman way of life with Turkish as the official language, the Greek judicial system was replaced by Turkish Tribunals and the Turks took over control of the harbours.

The liberation of Rhodes was a long time coming and when it did finally arrive, in 1922, the island exchanged Turkish masters for Italian.

## THE ITALIAN RULE (1912-1947)

The Italians arrived for a provisional occupation as liberators, they claimed, and not conquerors. Further assurances were given that there would be no interference in the Rhodian way of life or traditions. Free from the Turkish occupation and with all these fine assurances, the Italians were welcomed with open arms. Their promises were soon to prove empty.

At a congress of Dodecanese island delegates in June 1912, it was agreed on a vote the Aegean islands would return to Greece but that was not to be. The Treaty of Lausanne (October 1912) returned the Dodecanese to Turkey as soon as the Turks evacuated the Lybian provinces of Cyrenaica and Tripolitania. Events took a different turn when Turkey entered the 1914-18 war. The Italians argued that the Treaty of Lausanne lapsed with the renewed hostilities and laid claim to the Dodecanese islands which they occupied including Rhodes. This was formally acknowledged in the Treaty of London (April 1915). In the peace settlements of 1919-23, agreements were reached with the Italians to assign the Dodecanese back to Greece, with the exception of Rhodes.

Under the Italians the Rhodians suffered a period of oppression and tyranny especially with the rise of Mussolini and Fascism. Local government was dissolved and religious rites suppressed. The schools were taken over and Greek teachers replaced by Italians. The official language and the compulsory language of education became Italian. Land sales were enforced and sometimes expropriated for military use or for Italian immigrants and much was done to destabilise the social structure. On the other hand, money was injected into the economy and with skilled administrators the island saw some benefits. New roads were built and lavish public buildings many of which can still be seen today. They also excavated a number of the sites of antiquity and indulged in a good deal of restoration, but not all of it well done.

Italian occupation was exchanged for German occupation during World War II but it was eventually liberated by the British and in May 1947 was finally granted union with Greece.

# Rhodes Town

To many, medieval Rhodes Town is Rhodes. Admittedly, the old fortress town is the best preserved of its kind in Europe and a magnet which draws an endless stream of visitors but Rhodes Town is more than that, it is a place which offers something for everyone with a diversity of interest beyond the bastions of the old city walls. In the bustle of busy Mandraki Harbour sailing boats come and go while the colourful, teeming streets of modern Rhodes are perfect for those who shop until they drop. All this under the glare of the medieval ramparts looking on with silent envy.

Few towns know the date of their birth but Rhodes does. Built to form one economic and political centre, it was founded in 408BC and given the name *Damos Rodion* (City of Rodians). Until uniting to form the new city, Kamiros, Ialysos and Lindos had functioned as separate city states. Despite losing its political influence, Lindos was the only one of the three to retain importance, the others slipping gradually into obscurity as their populations transferred to the new city. Lindos continued as a major religious centre and thriving port, due in no small measure to its having the only natural harbour on the island and strong defences.

The present day site of Rhodes Town on the north-east promontory of the island, the ancients 'Pan's end', was chosen chiefly for its abundant water and harbours. A large triangular plain, it was bounded to the west and south by a range of low hills and open to the sea on the north and east. On the east side lay the three main harbours. The military port (Mandraki, much smaller now than it was then), great harbour (Emborio) and Akandia. Chains across the entrances to the first two harbours were an added protection. Two further harbours, to the west and south-east, brought the total to five but these have long since silted up. Traces of the solid piers, built to protect the harbours, can still be traced in the present day moles of St Nicholas and Myloi (windmills). These harbours, along with a securely protected naval yard, made Rhodes the best equipped port in the Aegean.

The new city of Rhodes had a very different architectural framework from the one we know today. During the time of its prime, in the second and third century BC, it is estimated to have had a population of up to 100,000, more than five times the size of the later medieval town. Rhodes Town was developed in the 'Hippodamean' style from a design attributed to the famous Hippodamus of Miletus. Based on a geometric pattern, this was a system of wide streets rising in straight lines from the harbours in the east to the west, and from north to south cutting each other at regular angles. Walls, 8 miles (13km) overall in length, formed a barrier on the landward side and apparently circled round to enclose the city. This latter information is found in an oration delivered by one Ailios Aristides to encourage the rebuilding of the city after the AD155 earthquake. 'But the first and foremost wonder that the eyes could not be sated with watching was the circle of the walls and their high and beautiful towers, looking straight as candles to those approaching by sea — '. Possibly an even more impressive sight than their medieval successors! There was the inevitable acropolis on St Stefanos' hill, modern Monte Smith, with the new Hellenistic city spreading from there down the hillside in the direction of the harbours. Some inscriptions found in the area of the present day castle, point to this having been the site of an ancient sanctuary of the sun god Helios. A site which could have existed long before the new city was built. The original area of St John's Church of the Knights, near the palace, was also known in medieval times as St Johannes Colossensis. It does not then seem too improbable that this was a possible site for the Colossus of Rhodes, the statue of Helios the sun god (page 33).

Little remains of the original city but recent excavations are helping to build up a better picture. Water was distributed to houses through terracotta pipes which have been found in great numbers beneath road surfaces. Of present day interest, lead pipes were little used for reasons of health, an effect which had been recognised in other cities

*preceding page: The three windmills at Mandraki Harbour have become a symbol of Rhodes Town*

# The Colossus of Rhodes

Tradition relates how Demetrios, after his defeat by the Rhodians in 305BC, requested his siege equipment be sold and the money used to erect a statue to their victory. Chares of Lindos, a pupil of Lysippos, was commissioned to execute this mammoth task. (Lysippos of Sikyon, was a sculptor who had been attached to the court of Alexander the Great. The 'School of Rhodes' for artists was founded under his influence.) His statue of the sun god Helios, begun in 304BC, took 12 years to complete and was crafted 'in situ', each section being cast in huge heaps of earth so that it was built up in stages.

When completed, the Colossus stood approximately 115ft (35m) high. Depictions for tourist consumption arise from a drawing of a statue straddling the harbour by the Belgian Rottier in 1826. This was based on a somewhat fanciful medieval notion as there are no records as to its pose or siting.

Regarded by the ancients as an outstanding technical and artistic achievement, the Colossus was considered one of the seven wonders of the world. Unfortunately, its period of glory was brief. The great earthquake of 227BC caused it to break at the knees and fall.

For nearly 900 years it lay untouched. Helios (Apollo) was apparently displeased with his statue and through his oracle at Delphi forbade its restoration. The Rhodians, afraid of dire consequences should they disobey such a request, obviously complied. Eventually, when Saracens plundered Rhodes in AD653, the bronze was transported across the sea and sold to a merchant from Edessa. It reputedly took 900 camels to transport the metal. The story was perpetuated even longer, with the said Colossus returning as Turkish cannonballs during the siege of AD1522.

of the time. The course of most of the ancient streets, especially outside the medieval walls, is little changed to this day. A traveller who visited Rhodes in AD1190 commented that most of the ancient buildings still stood.

Rhodes City lost its importance when the Romans, peeved with them for not willingly joining in their battle against Perseus (168BC), took back Caria and Lycia and granted free port status to Delos. This saw the beginning of the decline in Rhodes' influence. Left prey to marauders and the effects of earthquakes, especially the earthquake of AD155, Rhodes slipped into a steady decline. Its fortunes were not to rise again until the eleventh century, when it became a supply station for Crusaders on the way to the Holy Land.

Suddenly, Rhodes was back in favour as the importance of its strategic position became apparent to the developing commercial states of Western Europe. It then became a pawn in a wrestling match between Byzantium, the Genoese and Venetians. Forced out of Palestine by the failure of the Crusades, the Knights of St John set their sights on Rhodes as a new home. In 1306, they bought the island although it was to be a further 2 years before they secured full control.

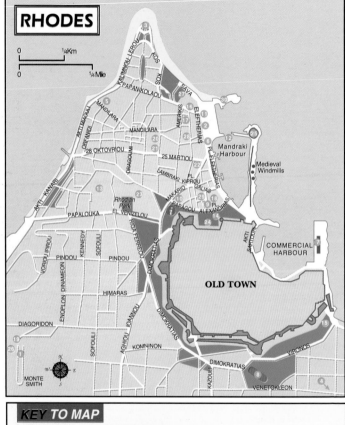

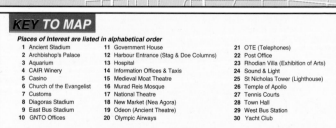

## KEY TO MAP

*Places of Interest are listed in alphabetical order*

| | | |
|---|---|---|
| 1 Ancient Stadium | 11 Government House | 21 OTE (Telephones) |
| 2 Archbishop's Palace | 12 Harbour Entrance (Stag & Doe Columns) | 22 Post Office |
| 3 Aquarium | 13 Hospital | 23 Rhodian Villa (Exhibition of Arts) |
| 4 CAIR Winery | 14 Information Offices & Taxis | 24 Sound & Light |
| 5 Casino | 15 Medieval Moat Theatre | 25 St Nicholas Tower (Lighthouse) |
| 6 Church of the Evangelist | 16 Murad Reis Mosque | 26 Tennis Courts |
| 7 Customs | 17 National Theatre | 27 Town Hall |
| 8 Diagoras Stadium | 18 New Market (Nea Agora) | 28 Town Hall |
| 9 East Bus Stadium | 19 Odeon (Ancient Theatre) | 29 West Bus Station |
| 10 GNTO Offices | 20 Olympic Airways | 30 Yacht Club |

*It is a pleasant stroll down the side of Rhode's Commercial Harbour,
adjacent to the city wall*

# The Knights Hospitallers of St John

The Knights stem from the nursing monks of a hospice founded by Italian merchants in the eleventh century. Known as Brother Hospitallers of St John of Jerusalem, their purpose was to tend Christian pilgrims visiting Jerusalem. Their taste for arms was probably fostered when they extended their care to providing an armed escort service. Fired by the desire to wage war on the 'infidel' after the first Crusade, they turned themselves into a military order while still retaining their role as carers of the sick. The forces of Saladin and their bitter rivalry with the Templars, also a military order, was to force them out of Jerusalem to seek a new base.

Only a noble of unblemished character and with Catholic parents could enter the Order as a future Knight. Vows of chastity, obedience and poverty were demanded and the noble could not become a fully fledged Knight before the age of 18. The Order consisted of three classes, a maximum of 600 Knights militant recruited from noble lineage, serving brothers as assistants and nurses and chaplains. The Knights tentacles reached far beyond the bounds of Rhodes and their influence stretched to the administration of their numerous estates in Europe and into every court.

Vanquished from Palestine, the Knights settled for a short time on Cyprus before purchasing Rhodes. It did not take them long to appreciate the islands merits as a permanent base. Over a period of years their fortifications gained a reputation as models of military architecture, especially the city walls. A powerful fleet of war galleys further enhanced that reputation. To ensure protection from the east they built fortresses on outlying islands, annexed to Rhodes, all of whom had at least one swift dispatch vessel. Thus, along with the thirty castles or so they erected or restored on the island, a strong line of communication was established to warn of imminent attack. As the reputation of the 'Knights of Rhodes' grew so did their coffers. Financed by their estates in Europe, their fortunes were given a boost when the Templars were suppressed in 1312 and some of their forfeited wealth and possessions passed to the Knights on Rhodes.

With the Knights came the great architectural changes still seen today. These took place in two periods; not by design but as the result of the siege of Mohammed II in 1480 and earthquakes in 1481. Until 1480 redevelopment was very much a local affair and did not attain the grandeur of the later period which was to last only 42 years but prove extremely productive. This was due in no small measure to the supervision of Grand Master d'Aubusson, who drafted in Western

Although nursing care was still part of the Order's duties, this aspect became blurred as their prime objective moved to defending the church against the 'infidel'. The hospital became the Knights' domain at the expense of the poor and sick, on which the Order was founded.

The Order was divided originally into seven 'tongues' (langues), France, Provence, Auvergne, Spain, Italy, Germany and England which later became eight with the subdivision of Spain into Aragon and Castile. The official language was French but Latin was used for manuscripts. Each group lived in an 'inn' under the leadership of a prior (pilier) and had particular responsibilities, for example, France directed all the Order's hospitals and Italy was Grand Admiral in command of the Knights' fleets. The tongues were also responsible for defending a section of the walls, known as 'curtains' (see medieval town plan page 42). A Grand Master was elected by the Knights to preside over the priors who constituted the Chapter of the Order. His tenure was for life and there were a total of nineteen grand masters. Not surprisingly, the majority were French as three of the tongues were French speaking. A political manoeuvre by a Spanish grand master was to split the Spanish tongue into Aragon and Castile and so increase the Spanish vote and influence.

When the Knights were finally defeated by the Turks in 1522 they negotiated a safe departure. It took them 7 years to find another home, Malta. As the Knights of Malta they succeeded in keeping the Turks out of the western Mediterranean, especially in 1565 when they were under attack for 4 months before help arrived. The beginning of the end for the Knights came after the Battle of Lepanto in 1571, when the Turks were defeated by a combined force of European powers assisted by the Order. Interest spread beyond the bounds of the Mediterranean, to the New World and Far East, and the Knights were left behind as other powers developed fleets of sailing vessels. By this time the English Order had ceased to exist, being disbanded when Henry VIII broke away from the church of Rome.

Their end came with the annexation of Malta by Napoleon in 1798 and the confiscation of their French assets after the Revolution. Despite such an ignominious end, their traditions live on in Britain in the form of the St John Ambulance Association.

expertise to oversee and build the Gothic style structures to a planned design.

Under the Knights, the walls were strengthened to withstand bombardment by increasingly sophisticated weaponry, their outer walls curved to deflect cannonballs. Gates were a weak link in the fortification. Of the original eight, some were blocked off or re-sited and a complicated double moat and drawbridge system constructed which can still be seen at the Amboise and Koskinou gates. The inner moat was purposefully left dry to deter the building of siege towers. Forts were constructed at the end of the harbour moles to increase protection. St Nicholas Tower guarding the naval harbour of Mandraki still stands. Little remains of the square Naillac Tower, destroyed in the nineteenth century, which along with the French Tower stood at the entrance to the Commercial Harbour (Emborio) with a heavy chain slung between. Fifteen windmills stood along the mole of the French Tower which retains the name of Mole of the Windmills, not to be confused with the three Mandraki windmills. Crowning these impressive fortifications was the Palace of the Grand Masters, a fortress within a fortress, built on the site of an ancient temple to Helios (later Apollo).

Compared with the size of the Hellenistic city, the medieval fortress city was much smaller. A low inner wall separated the Knights' quarters or Collachium (Kastellos), which housed all the buildings associated with their order, from the rest of the town (Bourg) where the merchants lived. The Knights barely had time to enjoy their new quarters before the ever-present Moslem threat erupted. Under Suleiman the Magnificent, the Turks mounted a siege on the island which lasted for 177 days before the Knights finally capitulated.

Despite a stay of 390 years, the Turks contributed little by way of new building. In fact, they inadvertently caused the destruction of prime medieval treasures in a spectacular explosion, which left many hundreds of people dead. A long forgotten cache of gunpowder, stored somewhere beneath the Palace of the Grand Masters and Church of St John when Suleiman the Magnificent captured Rhodes, exploded after lightning struck in the vicinity of the church and started a fire. The Church of St John was razed, the Inn of Germany completely disappeared and all that was left of the Palace of the Grand Masters was a burnt out shell.

Gradually, the medieval city began to take on an oriental look. Turkish elements, such as wooden balconies and window lattices, were added to the existing buildings and, with the addition of a minaret, churches were converted into mosques. The Turks did build some imposing mosques, including those of Suleiman and Retzep Pasha. They also built several *hammams* (public baths) but the only one in use now is the Mustafa Pasha *hammam*. Eastern type houses also appeared. These either opened onto the street or were entered through gardens or courtyards.

When the Turks arrived, they took over the Collachium and a large part of the Bourg allocating the eastern end to the Jews and expelling the Greeks. The Greeks could enter the city by day but had to leave, on pain of death, at night. As a result of this, new settlements developed outside the city walls along the remains of the ancient road network. The Greeks built six quarters, or 'Marasia', outside the city walls which

*The second-century BC carved head of the Sun God Helios, seen in the Archaeological Museum*

*View from St Nicholas mole of the Church of the Evangelist, modelled on the Knights' Church of St John*

still exist today; St Anastasia, St Anargyrous, St Nicholas, St George, Masari and Neochori. Fortunately, the 2 miles (4km) of city walls remained virtually untouched and this preservation was due in no small measure to the Turks using land immediately outside the walls as cemeteries.

After the Turks came the Italians in 1912. They were responsible for the reconstruction of the Palace of the Grand Masters, destroyed by the gunpowder explosion of 1856, and the Italian buildings fronting Mandraki Harbour. While in control, the Italians were prolific builders, restorers and excavators of ancient sites. Many of the Turkish embellishments, especially those tacked onto medieval buildings, were dismantled under their rule. Churches that had been changed into mosques were reconsecrated and the skyline robbed of many of its minarets. Much of the Italian legacy remains intact within Rhodes Town, including the deserted and forlorn looking Hotel des Roses near the Turkish cemetery. The Italians were to be ousted themselves in 1943 when German forces occupied the island.

Modern day Rhodes Town has burgeoned under the mantle of tourism, especially in the last 20 years. The Greeks love affair with concrete has manifested itself in the usual erosion of space, or so it seems, without yielding anything of architectural merit. No lessons seem to have been learnt even from as late as the Italian era. Fortunately, the medieval walls and Italianate buildings along Mandraki conceal this modern metropolis of narrow streets and clustered concrete buildings. In spite of its shortcomings, including the less than friendly 'take it or leave it' attitude now prevalent in high density tourist centres, Rhodes Town has much to offer the visitor. A medieval atmosphere, with a modern flavour, is more likely to be conjured up in the old city by those willing to stir themselves early or linger late into the evening under the stars.

Rhodes Town lies at the northern tip of the island. A finger of heavily developed land pointing along the imaginary line which divides the Aegean and Mediterranean seas. In this area are to be found most of the newer hotels. For a quieter more authentic ambience, it is worth seeking out the smaller, less sophisticated hotels tucked into the maze of streets in the old town. Besides hotels there is a plethora of pensions and rooms available yet, despite a seeming abundance of accommodation, Rhodes popularity with tour operators and an invasion of visitors during high season creates a scarcity. If a gourmet experience is essential to your stay then again, Rhodes can offer just about anything to satisfy most palates. Spring is a good time to visit but, come before 1 April and the tourist streets in the old city will still be closed and shuttered.

There is no substitute for exploring on foot. The four tours outlined below cover both the new and old towns. Apart from its harbour front and neglected Turkish cemetery, the main draw of the new town is its upmarket shopping. The old town bursts into life in summer and becomes the hub around which everything else revolves. Its maze of narrow streets, archways and courtyards invite exploration and promise a new discovery around every corner. Winter exposes a very different face when even the locals complain about the lack of things to do but, for those who wish to avoid the trappings of tourism, it is good time to come and wander at leisure.

A surprising plus point is the availability of clean and free WC's, also to be found in the museums. Traffic is banned from the old town, except to residents, while in the new, parking and one-way streets are a confusion in themselves. The best option for those with a car, staying outside the town, is to park in the suburbs and walk in. When entering a church or mosque, the usual rules of dress apply (ie no skimpy clothing), which includes shorts and sleeveless tops usually. In addition, should a mosque be entered, visitors are required to remove their footwear at the entrance. This is a practical ruling, to protect the carpets covering the floor on which the men sit for prayer.


## TOUR 1 • MEDIEVAL HIGHLIGHTS

A confusion of influences assail the senses on a walk through the old town. The stoic grandeur of the medieval fortress-like buildings seem at odds with the narrow alleyways and homespun architecture of the houses. Graceful minarets, rickety balconies, tranquil squares with fountains and shady trees still exude an oriental air. Blue glass eyes, to ward off evil, Loukouma and the names of many dishes in restaurants are all part of the Turkish legacy.

A visit to all or some museums is usually on everyone's list. Even if ancient remains do not excite, the Museum of Decorative Arts with its insight into life during the past couple of hundred years, will interest all the family. If time is pressing, and there is only time for one museum visit, save it for the Palace of the Grand Masters. The Exhibition of Archaeological Excavations, displaying finds from Pre-historic to Hellenistic times is clear, informative and above all fascinating. The palace closes at 3pm and admittance to the museum stops at 2.30pm but the exhibition demands much longer than half an hour.

From the taxi stand in Platia Rimini, head past the ranks of sponge sellers to enter the old town through the **Freedom Gate** (Pili Eleftherias). This narrow bridge has to cope with a steady stream of traffic, in both directions, as well as a swell of tourists. An early or later start will allow chance to observe the deer in their compound to the left or glorious curtains of bougainvillea cascading down the walls, without being swept along by the crowd.

Once inside, leaving the traffic to hurtle left out through the **Arsenal Gate**, head up the right-hand side of Platia Simis. The tour starts in the **Collachium**, the Knights-preserve. To the left are the remains of a

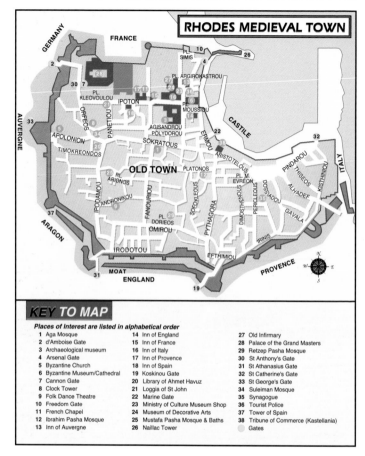

**RHODES MEDIEVAL TOWN**

KEY TO MAP

Places of Interest are listed in alphabetical order

1 Aga Mosque
2 d'Amboise Gate
3 Archaeological museum
4 Arsenal Gate
5 Byzantine Church
6 Byzantine Museum/Cathedral
7 Cannon Gate
8 Clock Tower
9 Folk Dance Theatre
10 Freedom Gate
11 French Chapel
12 Ibrahim Pasha Mosque
13 Inn of Auvergne
14 Inn of England
15 Inn of France
16 Inn of Italy
17 Inn of Provence
18 Inn of Spain
19 Koskinou Gate
20 Library of Ahmet Havuz
21 Loggia of St John
22 Marine Gate
23 Ministry of Culture Museum Shop
24 Museum of Decorative Arts
25 Mustafa Pasha Mosque & Baths
26 Naillac Tower
27 Old Infirmary
28 Palace of the Grand Masters
29 Retzep Pasha Mosque
30 St Anthony's Gate
31 St Athanasius Gate
32 St Catherine's Gate
33 St George's Gate
34 Suleiman Mosque
35 Synagogue
36 Tourist Police
37 Tower of Spain
38 Tribune of Commerce (Kastellania)
Gates

third-century BC Temple of Aphrodite and in front of this is a useful map showing the layout of the town. Further up the rise, on the left, facing partially onto Platia Argirokastrou, is the **Inn of Auvergne** built in 1507 and more recently restored. A Byzantine baptismal font serves as an unusual fountain in the Argirokastrou Square and heaps of cannonballs, from the Turkish siege of 1522, are displayed as decoration. One of the earliest buildings in the Collachium fronts the square, the colour and texture of its stonework softened by a tumbling mass of bougainvillea. This was originally the Palace of the Armeria, constructed under the Grand Master Roger de Pinsot in the fourteenth century, and the First Hospital of the Knights. It was also used by the Knights and Turks as an arsenal but today it enjoys a more peaceful

*The wide, bustling Sokratous Street, is the most famous and photographed in Rhodes old town*

role, it houses the offices of the Archaeological Institute of the Dodecanese and is where the first museum is located.

The **Museum of Decorative Arts**: an off-putting title for a delightful  and intimate Folk Art Museum where decorated tiles, intricately carved woodwork, brightly coloured Rhodian style pottery and exquisite needlework are elegant reminders of an earlier culture. A reconstruction of the interior of a traditional Rhodian house provides a good insight into everyday life. Even here, a Turkish influence can be detected. Many exhibits seem to originate from the island of Symi where women could appear well provided with rich dresses by owning just one long, sleeveless, elaborately embroidered 'gilet' to wear over a basic plain dress embroidered only round the neck, hem and sleeves.

Not much further up the street, again on the right, is the **Ministry of Culture Museum Shop**. For a piece of Greek history to take home, look no further. On sale are authentic casts of parts of friezes and funeral stele and replicas of ancient Greek jewellery. From hereon, souvenir shops jostle for attention with displays of gold and silver, leather, lace and the inevitable T-shirts.

On the opposite side of the road is the thirteenth century Byzantine **Church of St Mary** (Panagia tou Kastrou or Virgin of the Fort), which became the first cathedral of the Knights. A forced change of allegiance under Turkish rule saw its steeple converted into a minaret and renamed Enderoum. After a Christian massacre here in 1523 it became known to Rhodians as the 'red mosque'. Converted back again for use as a Christian church it has become a fitting home for the **Byzantine Museum** which contains an exhibition of well displayed Byzantine paintings and frescos in an atmospheric setting. One fresco has even been transferred from Halki and is displayed on the ceiling of the barrel vault.

The cobbled street Odos Ipoton, the 'Street of the Knights', rises up right to the Palace of the Grand Masters. For the moment though, continue into Platia Moussieo (Museum). Tucked back on the left is a bank, separated from the rather undistinguished **Inn of England** by a narrow street. A plaque on the wall of the Inn here is the only indication that the building is of any significance. Rebuilt to the original plan a century after its destruction in 1856, World War II again left it in need of repair. Of more interest are the eateries along the narrow alley which leads off the far left-hand corner of the square beyond the inn.

The impressive building to the right commands attention. This was the new Hospital of the Knights and their original *raison d'etre*. Begun in 1440, over the remains of a Roman building, it was not until the Grand Master d'Aubusson took charge over 40 years on that it was completed. It was built along similar lines to Byzantine hostelries. Eight plain arches support the façade, the only relief to the severe exterior being the decorative, recessed Gothic arch of the main gateway which lies beneath the projection of the chapel above. Unfortunately, the original wooden main gate found its way to Versailles when it was sold by the Turks in the nineteenth century. After the Knights' departure it was used variously as a hospital then ignobly as a barracks. Skilfully restored by the Italians and again after suffering bomb damage during World War II it now serves as the **Archaeological Museum**. The entrance opens into a courtyard, surrounded by a galleried upper story accessed by an outside stairway. Stone fragments and stacks of cannonballs, relics from various sieges, lie on the ground and a first-century BC marble statue of a crouching lion takes centre spot. Upstairs is the large room which was the Infirmary Ward. What the small windowless rooms down the sides were used for is open to conjecture, possibly isolation wards or maybe wardrobes. Pilgrims came here for treatment until the needs of the Knights themselves became paramount. When this happened, the vow of poverty seems to have been conveniently forgotten! Simple wooden beds were replaced by beds decked with brocaded canopies and nothing less than silver plate was good enough to eat off. Some imagination is needed to conjure up what this bare room must have looked like fully furnished.

Medieval gives way to an earlier era in other rooms along the gallery. It is difficult not to admire the art of the sculptor in Hellenistic times and the marble statuette of Aphrodite bathing, an adaptation of an earlier first century BC sculpture, is a fine example. There is also another sculpted Aphrodite from the third century BC more commonly known as the Marine Venus after being hauled out of the sea nearly 70 years ago. It is this sculpture which inspired the title of Lawrence Durrell's book *Reflections on a Marine Venus* about his life on Rhodes. A second-century BC head, from a statue of the Sun God Helios driving his chariot in the sky, still has the holes where iron spikes for the sun's rays would have been positioned. It is thought that this was sited in the Temple to Helios. Grave stele, as here, provide an insight into the everyday life of ordinary people of the time. One from Kamiros depicts a fifth-century BC bas-relief of a girl saying good-bye to a dead mother and another, erected by Damokles to his dead wife Kalliaista, shows her seated in front of her maid. Besides these gems there are many funerary objects which is not too surprising, as most of the information gleaned about this early period comes from ancient cemeteries. Pottery figures strongly, especially Geometric and there are also some mosaics.

Leaving the Collachium with its austere façades, it is time for a complete change of scene. What greater contrast can there be than the Turkish bazaar atmosphere of Sokratous Street! Continuing in the same direction, outdoor tables on the square at Polydorou are invitingly placed for the thirsty visitor and it is tempting to pause and watch the world go by. Moving on through the square, **Sokratous** is ✳ not difficult to miss. Its wide bustling street, reminiscent of its central role in the old bazaar rises up towards Suleiman Mosque. With the projecting wooden balconies (*sachnisi*) of its Turkish style buildings, this is the most famous and photographed street in the old town. A short diversion left here leads into Platia Ipokratous, beyond which is the medieval courthouse and stock exchange, the Kastellania, and close by the impressive Marine Gate.

Wandering up Sokratous could take a long time. Colour spills onto the street as traders entice with their assortment of wares, ikons, replica helmets, embroidery, carpet weaving, ceramics and leather sandals all clamouring for attention. Pastry shops and cafés seduce the foot weary while the lure of shady alleyways suggest more peaceful oases. An arch jutting out into the street, the Aga Mosque, has so far restricted the view ahead but from hereon the **Suleiman Mosque** comes into better focus. Minus its minaret it no longer dominates the skyline on this approach as seismic activity in 1991 so weakened its structure it had to be dismantled for the sake of safety. Fortunately, there are plans afoot for its restoration but when is the moot point in question. The loss of the minaret has certainly diminished the character of this otherwise fascinating street.

Closer inspection of the Suleiman Mosque reveals serious neglect and it is no longer open to the public. Built on the site of an earlier Church of the Apostles, it was erected in honour of the Sultan after his conquest of Rhodes in 1522 and rebuilt in 1808. Now, one can only peer through the locked gates at its rotting wood and crumbling pink cement to imagine its former magnificence. The pink colour on many old buildings is not paint but a special pink cement used for waterproofing on floors, roofs, domes and walls. Do not continue up past the mosque but go right in front of it along Panetiou. The commanding walls of the Palace of the Grand Masters loom ahead. On the left are excavations of medieval buildings behind which is the Turkish school constructed on the site of the Conventual Church of St John destroyed in the 1856 gunpowder explosion. A fragment of wall being the sole remains. Built in a plain architectural style during the fourteenth century it contained the tombs of the Knights, remnants of which are found in the Knights Hospital. Pass the top of the 'Street of the Knights' to enter the palace environs. At the end of the street is Platia Kleovoulou and the restored **Loggia of St John** which, when the Knights were in residence on the island, connected the palace with the Church of St John. Two round towers announce the entrance to the palace, its large pointed door being one of the parts preserved from the original building.

The **Palace of the Grand Masters** stands on the highest part of the Collachium, and was built on the probable site of the Sanctuary of Helios in the fourteenth century. Helios was the original sun god on Rhodes but he appears to have been supplanted at some later time by Apollo who was also a sun god as well as sometime god of light, poetry, music etc. The role of gods being manipulated by different peoples to suit their personal requirements. Designed as a fortress in its own right with underground storerooms to withstand siege, it served as the Grand Masters' residence and the hub of the Knights' activities. Although it survived the Turkish siege of 1522 little damaged, its use as a prison and the earthquake of 1851 hastened structural decline. The gunpowder explosion and fire 5 years later, coupled with removal of stone for other building work by the Turks, effectively sealed the fate of this once commanding edifice.

Left to languish for the next 80 years, it took a new master to restore its fortunes when, under the Italians in the 1930s, it was rebuilt as an

*(above) Views from the* son et lumière *gardens lend a different perspective to the Palace of the Grand Masters (below) The inner courtyard of the palace*

intended summer residence for Victor Emmanuel III and Mussolini. The exterior is supposed to follow the style of the old building with the interior adapted more to modern day requirements with electricity and central heating. Even camouflaged lifts were installed so as not to appear incongruous in such a setting. Ostentation was more a prerequisite than taste when it came to interior design, or so it seems. The lavish style extending to the use of Roman and Byzantine columns and importation of some fine Roman and Early Christian mosaics from Kos.

The entrance to the main body of the palace is up the sweep of stairs to the left, opposite the pay desk immediately on entering. Inscriptions near this entrance appertain to the Italian Fascist regime and to Greek Independence gained in 1947. Ahead is the inner courtyard with its display of Roman statuary and off this courtyard is a snack bar and the entrance to the special exhibition within the palace of ancient local finds. The exhibition covers the period from prehistoric times to the Hellenistic City and includes some excellent mosaics. It is well annotated and displayed and time spent absorbing the information in here really helps to recreate the living and breathing Rhodes of old. Climb the stairs to wander through the corridors and spacious rooms open to the public where a combination of seemingly wall to wall mosaics, statues, Italian Renaissance carving and scant furnishings add to the sterile atmosphere. This mix of periods lie uneasily together. Views from the windows over the town and gardens give a different perspective as does a walk along the old city walls.

Walking the walls is an excellent way to appreciate them as a tremendous feat of fortification. It also provides a superb overview of the old town which helps to put the layout into perspective. Only accessible on Tuesdays and Saturdays at 2.45pm but often open from 2.30pm. Tickets at the entrance to the palace. The unguided walk starts up the steps and through the small **Cannon Gate** off the outer courtyard. Covering only about a third of its original length, the walk passes along the 'Curtains' defended by Auvergne, Aragon and England, in that order, ending at the **Koskinou Gate**. Descend into Efthimiou and follow right then round left along Dimosthenous to **Platia Evreon Martiron**, the Square of the Jewish Martyrs which is easily identified by its tasteless modern fountain of bronze seahorses. The square was renamed in memory of the remaining Jewish population, who were deported from this spot to concentration camps when the Germans arrived in 1943. Only a few Jewish families live in the old town now out of a population numbering 6,000 before 1939, a fortunate 4,000 of whom emigrated at the outset of war. Close by, in Dosiadou, can be located the synagogue. The next street out of the square on the left leads to the **Ibrahim Pasha Mosque** and very pleasant Platanos Square, reputed to have been used as a place of execution by the Turks with the Demerli Mosque lying a little further along. This is also a good area for exploring the numerous alleyways with less touristy shops. Sokratous lies just north of here.

Leaving the palace, go left down **Ipoton**, the 'Street of the Knights', one of the best preserved medieval streets in existence. Besides being the main route from the palace to the port through the Collachium, it is the location of the inns of the various tongues. The present day pristine appearance of the cobbled street is thanks in no small measure to the Italians, who dismantled the Turkish addition of rickety wooden balconies to restore the late medieval architecture. Restoration alone though does not bring buildings to life. Now used mainly as offices, it lacks the buzz of habitation and shows itself for what it has become — a museum piece, nevertheless, it is an impressive street. Even before it gained its medieval mantle it was an ancient route to the port. From this angle, the first point to catch the eye is an arch spanning the street. The **Inn of Spain** lies to the right either side of the arch and the room above the arch belongs to it while opposite is the later built, more elaborate, **Inn of Provence**.

Lower down on the left is the small fourteenth-century **Church of Agia Triada** (Holy Trinity) attached to the Inn of France which was converted by the Turks to a mosque called Han-Zade and before the chapel the house belonging to its chaplain. Well down the street now, reach the richly ornamented **Inn of France** on the left where the coats of arms of France, with its three lilies and royal crown, and the Grand Master d'Aubusson with its cardinal's hat can be seen in a carved frame, dated 1495. The building across the road, next to the hospital, had connections with the Inn of Spain. Finally, near the bottom of the street on the left, is the **Inn of Italy** with its exterior showing simpler lines than those of the Inn of France.

## TOUR 2 • THE OLD QUARTER

A voyage of discovery lies awaiting intrepid explorers willing to explore the maze of alleyways and streets of the old town. Medieval and Turkish styles blend to create a unique and intriguing atmosphere within the confines of the old walled town. Tucked away in here are countless small workshops where skilled craftsmen still practice their art in much the same way as their ancestors. Although this tour follows a defined route, it is only a guideline and forays where the fancy leads add to the enjoyment. Keeping a map to hand can help, even if only to make sure not too many ever decreasing circles are tramped although a number of principal streets assist in making some order out of seeming chaos. Sokratous leads down from the mosque of Suleiman towards the harbour, continuing as Aristotelous then Pindarou as it skirts round parallel with the Commercial Harbour. A rough grid of streets south of Sokratous is formed by Ipodamou, Fanouriou, Pythagora and Omirou. Many of the small hotels and pensions are to be found in the tortuous network of narrow lanes within this grid. The Bourg shows an equally fascinating face by night when murmuring voices, clinking glasses, bouzouki music, soft shadows and twinkling lights change leafy platias into magical enclaves. This walk could take all day if a lunch in ambient surroundings, haggling over souvenirs and frequent pit stops for a drink is part of the equation.

Enter the old town via the **d'Amboise Gate** off Dimokratias. There is no mistaking the narrow entrance road lined with lace and souvenir stalls. With a swirl of activity going on all around, the magnificence of the gate itself is easily overlooked. Entry through this early sixteenth-century gate, one of the most impressive of all the gates, allows for an appreciation of the complicated defensive structure of the fortifications. Through the gate, a gauntlet of artists all too willing to draw your portrait, encourage an audience along the shaded walled road of the inner fortifications.

Once out of the confines of the walls, the rich tapestry begins to unfold. Restaurants and souvenir shops compete for attention but stopping along here for a drink might surprise the unwary. The result of a casual beer order could be an outsize trumpet-shaped glass of German beer, containing enough liquid to slake the thirst of a few. By now, the **Clock Tower** (To Roloi) will probably have captured attention. This offers the highest viewpoint in town. It was built in 1852 on the site of a previous tower and formed a corner of the wall which ran parallel with Ipoton to the port, separating the Collachium from the Bourg. The entrance price includes a soft drink or coffee.

Head across the top of Sokratous past the mosque of Suleiman (Tour 1) into Ipodamou. On the right is the Turkish **Library of Ahmet Havuz**, whose collection includes a chronicle of the siege of 1522 and two illuminated Korans of the fifteenth and sixteenth centuries. Immediately, the narrow cobbled street transports the visitor into a different age blanking out the hustle and bustle of the main tourist thoroughfare. Arches, protection against earthquakes, bridge the street, enticing alleyways, flower decked courtyards all exude a more tranquil air. Even the tourist shops become less intrusive. Divert left along Arhelaou, by the Symposium Garden Restaurant, to **Platia Arionos** and the Turkish Baths. Dominated by the Mustafa Pasha Mosque and baths of the same name, the square provides another opportunity to sit at one of the cafés and absorb the atmosphere. This Turkish bath (*hammam*) still functions, despite bomb damage during World War II, and subsequent renovation work is difficult to detect to the non expert (see box page 52).

For some excellent Greek dancing, an evening visit to the **Nelly Dimoglou Theatre** on Andronikou, behind the baths, is a must. Performances take place nightly, except Saturdays and Sundays, from May to October but the gardens are open every day. Return to Ipodamou to continue down the street. A stack of wood, piled against the outside wall, announces the shop of Dimitri Tsipillos. His bread is

*Portrait artists line the route inside d'Amboise Gate*

*A tranquil corner of old Rhodes Town*

## Mustafa Pasha Turkish Baths or Hammam

The original baths were built in 1558, during the early days of the Turkish occupation, and updated 200 years later when Mustafa Pasha built the mosque next door. This upgrade raised them to such a level of sophistication that they attracted visitors from the Ottoman mainland. Not only were they used for cleansing, they were also great meeting places as, centuries before, the Roman baths had been. To some extent they still function in much the same way today except that the main users are Greek with the Turks and tourists making up the minority. Worth a visit if only for a peep into a world little changed by the passage of time.

Men and women go their separate ways once through the doors. Decorative and plain marble is used to full effect inside and a good level of cleanliness maintained. The coolness of the changing cubicles contrasts sharply with the humidity level on the far side of a weighted door. Plunged into a maze of cubicles with bath or shower it is easy to become disorientated. The grand central room, with its domed ceiling, takes on an ethereal quality when its marble opulence is viewed through a steamy mist. Here, cold tap water is provided in individual carved marble water troughs. Amazingly, the water is still heated by the original log fire system, whose insatiable appetite must have consumed acres of olive trees down the centuries, and distributed along a network of pipes under the floor. A visit here is an experience in itself and stimulates a feeling of *joie de vivre* — try it!

still cooked the old fashioned way in the *fournos* but ensure arrival by lunchtime for, after an early morning start, he's more than ready for the afternoon siesta. Be sure to buy a *tiropitta* — they're delicious! The main advantage, for the customer, of a small oven is the steady stream of fresh bread. On approaching the walls ahead turn left, opposite number 46. (This route does not go past the St Nicholas Hotel, just after this turn off point, but it looks an inviting place to stay.) An intriguing wend through a narrow alleyway leads onto Omirou, emerging by the Ancient Market Garden Bar. Continue left along the street. There are better opportunities for sideways exploration and capturing a real flavour of the old town in this area.

Pass the end of Fanouriou, by Hotel Paris, to shortly turn left through an archway into **Platia Dorieos** with its domed fountain which makes a great setting for eating out under the trees. Tucked into a corner, and almost masked by a taverna, is the old Byzantine Church of Agios Fanourios but dominating the square is the **Retzep Pasha Mosque**, one of the most striking of all the Turkish buildings. To regain Fanouriou, cross the square to the left, from the entry point,

then turn right. **Fanouriou** is one of the oldest streets in the old town ✳
and can be better appreciated at this lower end. As the street rises up
towards the Collachium, an increase in souvenir shops announces the
return to the tourist heart. Emerge onto Sokratous by the Aga Mosque.

## TOUR 3 • MANDRAKI AND SHOPPING

Most of the new town has developed since the Italian occupation of
1912. The added impetus of tourism, especially during the past 20
years, has greatly accelerated development even further. Besides
being the shopping, administrative and business quarter, the northern
tip also contains most of the hotels and revolves around the tourist
industry. Mandraki Harbour is part of this quarter and a buzzing
meeting place for locals and tourists alike. To the west, especially on
the slopes of Monte Smith, are to be found leafy suburbs with larger
houses and villas while the south has the densest population and the
south-east most of the light industry. This too is the location of the
CAIR (KAIR) winery which is only open to visitors for wine tasting on
an organised tour (see feature box page 58-59). If plans to develop the
whole of the seafront here into a marina come to fruition, the winery
will completely transfer its operation to its new plant near Koskinou.

Although this tour concentrates on the northern section, a walk
round the outside of the old town walls is not without interest, nor a
walk or drive down the Lindos road to Rodini Park where the famous
Rhodes 'School of Rhetoric' was located. The wooded park was
designed and laid out by the Italians who populated it with deer and
peacocks. According to legend, the Delphic oracle urged the introduc-
tion of deer as a means of ridding the island of snakes but, when the
Italians arrived, all signs of deer had disappeared. Unfortunately, as
with much of the Italian legacy, neglect has taken its toll and the deer
have been long gone from the park. Depleted almost to extinction on
the island, only a few deer remain in the moat of the old town and in
a pen on Profitis Ilias. Also in the vicinity is a large Hellenistic rock
tomb, wrongly named 'tomb of the Ptolemies'.

Breakfast in the **New Market** (Nea Agora) makes a fitting start to ✳
this tour, as most local activity starts early. Using Rimini Square as the
starting point, and before heading for Mandraki, wander into the lush
gardens beneath the castle walls where the *son et lumière* is held. The
flowers here create a riot of colour, softening the gaunt crenellated
walls of the palace towering above. Its never too early for coffee, so it
is straight to the harbour front and the New Market. An irregular
seven sided construction built by the Italians in the Turkish style, this
building displays an unusual departure from the more severe lines of
their other building work. Round the outside are crowded numerous
snack bars, cafés and all manner of small shops selling herbs, spices,
nuts, olives and duty free wines and spirits. Rhodes is a duty free
island and spirits are cheap. Inside the huge and colourful tree shaded

courtyard, fresh fruit and vegetable stalls, butchers, tourist paraphernalia and cafés combine in a kaleidoscope of constant activity. The large centrepiece has a dual function, fish market above and underneath, free WC's. Most of the fish market activity seems to take place around 8am, with the fresh catch spilling out into the courtyard area. *Tiropitta, souvlakia* and pizza snacks are readily available from kiosks, especially those hot from the oven at the kiosk in the exit to Platia Alexandrias. The smaller market cafés provide good value for a quick breakfast or snack (see box page 57) Newspapers of all nationalities can be bought under the main gateway onto Mandraki. More sophisticated cafés, with a price to match, line the Mandraki frontage and offer more comfortable seats but the accompanying exhaust fumes, noise and crush of people may not be to everyone's taste. On the plus side, the coffee is good and the cakes...! Try the Greek *ekmek* which is particularly indulgent and delicious but very different from the original Turkish meaning of the word; bread.

❋ Busy **Mandraki Harbour**, a name derived from its shape meaning 'sheepfold', is crammed to capacity with sea craft during the summer. Besides use as an international yachting marina, the harbour accommodates local ferry and excursion boats including hydrofoils while larger ferries and cruise ships dock in the Commercial Harbour further south. A stroll along the harbour wall past the three windmills, where grain was milled for cargo boats, to **St Nicholas Tower**, now a lighthouse and chapel, provides a clear overview of the waterfront. The view is thwarted somewhat by a forest of bobbing, jangling masts. One of the best vantage points is from the narrow channel at the harbour entrance, especially after 9am when a mass exodus of excursion boats clears the waterfront. Two bronze statues of a stag and doe guard the harbour entrance. The doe replacing a statue of an Italian she-wolf which now resides in the grounds of the Palace of the Grand Masters.

In many ways, Mandraki is the link between the old town and the new. This spacious frontage is where the Italians chose to construct a new commercial quarter. Designed with a mix of Venetian, Gothic and Arabic elements, these monumental public buildings dominate the shoreline. On the seaward side of the road is the **Church of the Evangelist**, built in 1925 on the model of the Knights' Church of St John in the old town which was destroyed in the explosion of 1856. Next to the church is the **Archbishop's Palace** and then the former **Governor's Palace**, now Government House (Nomarkia), constructed in a more photogenic Venetian-Gothic style, whereas a Mussolini square style was used for the Town Hall, Post Office and National Theatre. Fashionable comment derides the tasteless grandeur of these honey-coloured buildings but, they at least provide a better foil for the medieval citadel than the angular mass of soulless concrete they mask.

North of Mandraki, off Platia Koundourioti, is the private Nautical Club and the start of the public beach. The coarse sand and shingle beach stretches round the point of Akrotiri Ammou (Sandy Beach) known also as Kumburnu Point. There is plenty of activity on these beaches in summer and changing facilities are available at the Elli Club for a small admission fee. The regimented rows of coloured beach umbrellas, all angled the same way, tell of the persistent breeze along

# Shopper's Guide

Rhodes is a mecca for bargain hunters and lives up to its reputation as a shopper's paradise. Most items are cheaper here than anywhere else in Greece due to special tax concessions conferred on the island when it was united with Greece in 1947. Spirits are definitely a good buy, with prices in the shops lower than the duty free shop at the airport and it pays to buy now rather than at departure. Choose from ready-to-wear designer labelled clothes or have them tailor-made within a matter of days from bargain fabrics, which include genuine Harris tweed and cashmere, and also leather and silk. Leather shoes are a good buy and the traditional soft leather boots can be made to measure. Handmade jewellery is a speciality in silver or 18-carat gold which is usually sold by weight, the price depending on current market rates. Umbrellas are everywhere and it is possible to buy one for every conceivable occasion. Sponges feature strongly in tourist areas (see Symi Chapter 9) and other good buys are herbs, spices and local honey. Add to all this a bewildering array of local handicrafts, pottery, olive wood carving, metal craft, embroidery and weaving and there is enough to keep the most ardent shopper occupied for many a day.

Bargaining is possible, especially in the souk-like atmosphere of the old town, and price reductions possible in jewellers but usually only on a cash payment basis.

the west coast. Moving west along Papanikolaou, the **Murad Reis Mosque** watches over a secluded backwater that was once the cemetery for the Turkish elite. Murad Reis himself was a prominent pirate killed during the Turkish siege of 1522 and his tomb is the circular mausoleum next to the mosque. Carved turbans top headstones of men while those for women are sharp-angled stone. Despite the air of obvious neglect, a dignified atmosphere still prevails where eucalyptus shade the graves of the many Moslem notables, including a Shah of Persia, which are transformed by carpets of white *Cyclamen persicum* in spring.

Leave this reminder of another age along Sava, in the direction of the sea. Still making for the point along the shoreline, pass the closed and shuttered Hotel des Roses; yet another abandoned Italian building. The **Aquarium** (Enidrio), its more grandiose title being the Hydrobiological Institute, sits in splendid isolation on the northernmost tip of the island and entrance to the subterranean grotto is behind the main building. In an attempt to simulate the seabed, fish found locally are displayed in tanks along the walls of a narrow twisting passageway while dried and pickled specimens of sword-fish, sharks and a whale can be viewed in separate rooms. A good place to go on a rainy day or to escape the heat.

Now for shopping! (see box page 55) From the Aquarium head directly south through Platia Vas. Pavlou, across Papanikolaou into Grivas. The network of streets between here and Octovriou is the tourist heartland of bars, restaurants and shops. An inelegant collection by day but lively by night! If lunch calls, Mollye's on Dragoumi and Les Arcs Bistro, off Dragoumi behind the San Antonio Hotel, serve good food and also cater for vegetarians. For more upmarket shopping go east along Mandilara to Amerikis then head south. On Amerikas and 25th Martiou are what pass as department stores on Rhodes. Make for Platia Cyprus (Kiprou) down Lambraki, a central point for banks and the more chic establishments. Designer label fashions and shoes sit comfortably alongside discreet and alluring displays of gold. Why umbrellas figure so strongly is a mystery, but there is no shortage of choice from fancy and frivolous to sombre and serviceable. A decade ago, fur products shared the umbrellas prominence but, due to current lack of demand, these outlets have shrunk considerably. Interspersed between these high-class retailers are some equally stylish cafés. Amongst them Cafe Central, where it is possible to escape the ubiquitous 'Nes' in favour of filter coffee, expresso or even capuccino and to tempt the palate is a variety of home-made cakes and pastries including 'Xaloumates' (*haloumates*), a cheese pie made with the less salty Cypriot haloumi cheese and not feta.

The triangle bounded by Averof, Papagou and Platia Cyprus has been pedestrianised, making it very pleasant for browsing or just sitting where a small enclave of Turkish style houses with wooden balconies has been preserved.

# Wine & Dine in Rhodes Town

'Spoilt for choice' is an epithet which springs to mind when considering the fare on offer in Rhodes Town. True gastronomes would need a very long holiday to sample all the delights on offer. Below are listed just fourteen choices for starters ranging from medium to expensive.

## British

*Mollye's*
25 Ionis Dragoumi
Home made steak pies and all things traditional including vegetarian dishes.

*The Yorkshire Diner*
45 Orfanidou & 28 Akti Miaouli
Sunday roast and other specialities.

## Danish

*Dania*
3 Iroon Polytechniou
A good cold plate selection tops full menu.

## Greek

*Salt & Pepper*
76 M Petridi
Traditional Greek food with best *mezedes* in town.

*Kamares Taverna*
15 Ag Fanouriou
Traditional dishes in traditional surroundings.

*Alexis*
18 Sokratous
A chance to sample some different fish dishes.

## Greek & French

*Les Arcs Bistro* 16
Konstantopedos: good selection of delicious dishes including vegetarian dishes.

## International

*Blue Lagoon*
2 25th March
Gourmet food and wine.

*Kon-Tiki Floating Restaurant*
In Mandraki harbour
Mouth-watering menu to suit all tastes.

*Symposium*
3 Archelou & 21 Ipodamou
Full cuisine including extensive sea food menu.

## Italian

*La Famiglia*
25 Ionos Dragoumi
Original Italian cooking.

## Italian-French

*Cleo's*
17 Ag Fanouriou
Closed Sunday: featuring the best of Italy and France.

## Mexican

*El Corazon*
27 Orfanidou
Hot and spicy, unique on Rhodes.

## Indian

*Shere Khan*
52 Orfanidou
Authentic Indian cooking with curries galore!

## ⫪ TOUR 4 • MONTE SMITH

A visit to Rhodes Town would not be complete without a trip up the hill of Agios Stefanos, better known as Monte Smith, named after the English Admiral Sir Sidney Smith, who kept watch on the Napoleonic fleet from there in 1802. This was the second-century BC site of the ancient acropolis, excavated and restored, in part, by the Italians. Very little remains of the once magnificent **Temple of Apollo**, but a small **Theatre** and the **Stadium** have been restored. Views over the town and across the water to Asia Minor are an unexpected bonus on this trip.

If the 20 to 30 minute walk up in the heat does not appeal, there is always a taxi or the regular blue bus which leaves from Mandraki waterfront. Do not forget to buy a prepaid ticket, also one for the return if required, from the kiosk by the bus stop which is validated in the machine on the bus.

From Rimini Square head up Papagou, into Dimokratias then right up Venizelou, signposted Acropolis of Rhodes. Follow the signs from here to the large car parking area below the remains. First to catch the eye are the three columns from the Temple of Apollo, re-erected in a somewhat piecemeal fashion and which look better viewed from a

---

# The CAIR (KAIR) Winery

The Company Agricultural Industry of Rhodes was started by the Italians in 1928, although the island has just celebrated 2,400 years of wine making. Now Greek owned and operated, the company produced a special white wine, Rodos 2400, to celebrate that milestone in history. A story from those early days tells how the Cretans, jealous of Rhodes' fame for high quality wine, copied Rhodian amphorae in an attempt to pass off their own wine as Rhodian.

To eliminate poorer quality grapes, vineyards on the Lindos side of the island, where the climate is too hot and dry, were destroyed and growing is now concentrated on the western side, around Embonas. Here many small vineyards are located in specific cooler microclimates where granite stones in the soil help by increasing humidity which in turn improves the flavour. Athiri, a very old local variety of white grape, is grown in vineyards on lower slopes below Embonas while mountain regions produce a better quality of red grape. Vineyards are specially selected for the quality of grapes used under each specific label and are constantly monitored.

Wine is produced on two sites. The original site, in Rhodes Town, produces Chevalier, Ilios and Retsina while the remaining labels now come from the new plant near Koskinou, where the latest technology is employed.

*The restored ancient ruins atop Monte Smith*

**CAIR labels include:-**

*Ilios:* Dry white from the Athiri grape.

*Chevalier de Rhodes:* Dry red from the Mandilaria. Said to be the same wine drunk by the 'Knights'. An indifferent red wine but the one mainly on offer in tavernas.

*Platoni:* A white, rose or red table wine from the Athiri and Mandilaria grapes.

*Moulin:* A white, rose, red, dry and semi-dry table wine. Produced from a mix of varieties including Cabernet Sauvignon and Grenache. The semi-dry white and rose, with a light, delicate flavour are particularly palatable with a meal or on their own.

*Rodos 2400:* A dry white from the Athiri grape.

*Arxontiko (Château):* A dry red wine from a mix of grapes. Lovers of red wines will appreciate the subtle hint of blackcurrant — best of the reds!

*Muscat de Rhodes:* A sweet white wine of the Moschato variety.

*Amandia:* A sweet red wine.

*Retsina:* Natural resin and the Athiri grape combine to make this an excellent lightly resinated crisp white wine.

*CAIR Brut & Demi-Sec:* A very drinkable sparkling wine from the Athiri grape.

*Nisiotikos:* Available in large as well as standard size bottles, this white, rose or red wine is ideal for general use.

distance. The small reconstructed 800 seat Theatre, more likely Odeon, sits beneath the site of the temple. Only the orchestra and three seats remain from the original structure, which was probably used for events associated with the cult of Apollo and maybe by the Rhodian School of Rhetoric. A much larger theatre is thought to have been sited elsewhere on the same hill. On the left is the reconstructed stadium of which again only a few rows, in the middle of the curve, are original. To the east of the stadium lay a Gymnasium but little tangible evidence survives. The Temple of Apollo sits on a platform above the huge retaining wall behind the theatre, approached by a flight of steps, and excavations close by are the remains of a fountain house and possible Nymphaia, for the worship of nymphs. To the north, foundations of a Temple to Zeus and Athena Polias have been revealed. Return down Voriou Ipirou for spectacular views over the town.

# *Additional Information*

## *Places to Visit in Rhodes*

**Art Gallery**
Open: Monday to Saturday 8am-2pm. Closed Sunday.

**Aquarium**
Subterranean display of local fish and also preserved specimens.
Open: Daily 9am-4.30pm.

**Archaeological Museum**
Mycenaean to Roman exhibits.
Open: Tuesday to Sunday 8.30am-3pm. Closed Monday.

**Byzantine Museum. Panagia Kastrou Exhibition**
Byzantine & Post-Byzantine Ikons.
Open: Tuesday to Sunday 8.30am-3pm. Closed Monday.

**Exhibition of Archaeological Excavations in the Palace of the Grand Masters**
Details last 40 years of local excavations.
Open: Tuesday to Sunday 8.30am-2.30pm. Closed Monday.

**Greek Folk Dances by Nelly Dimoglou**
Traditional Greek Dances
7 Andronikou
Nightly in high season, Monday to Friday only from 9.20-11pm.

**Monte Smith**
Temple of Apollo, Ancient Stadium & Theatre
Open access.

**Museum of Decorative Arts**
Folklore exhibits from Dodecanese Islands.
Open: Tuesday to Sunday 8.30am-3pm. Closed Monday.

**Palace of the Grand Masters**
Open: Tuesday to Sunday 8.30am-3pm. Closed Monday.

**Son et Lumière**
English language times.
Monday and Tuesday. 8.15pm; Wednesday, Friday & Saturday. 9.15pm; Thursday 10.15pm.

**To Rolio (The Clock Tower)**
Open: daily in season.

## Turkish Baths
Platia Arionos
Open: Tuesday 1-7pm and
Wednesday to Saturday 7am-7pm.
Take your own soap & towel.

## Walk Around the Walls
Starts from the Palace of the Grand
Masters every Tuesday and
Saturday at 2.45pm.

## *Useful Information*

### Transport
*Buses* radiate out from Rhodes
Town from the East and West bus
stations close to Mandraki. Local
buses run from Mandraki waterfront. Timetables available from
the Tourist Offices and bus kiosks.
See Fact File.

The following town buses leave
every 30minutes.
N3 to Rodini Park between 6am-9pm.
N5 to Monte Smith between
5.50am-9pm.
Buy tickets before boarding the bus
at the kiosk.

*Boats and Hydrofoils*
Daily excursions and ferries to
other islands and Piraeus. Check
travel agencies for details.

## *Accommodation*

### Hotels
* = Open all year.
Rhodes Town is packed with hotels,
apartments and rooms of all catego-
ries, including a De Luxe hotel, far
too many to be listed here. Below is a
selection of a few from De Luxe down
to C class. Further information can
be obtained from the Rodos Hotel
Association, PO Box 287, Rodos,
Greece ☎ (0241) 26446/27292 or the
Greek National Tourist Organisation,
(address on page 62) but do not rely
on their accommodation lists being
up to date.

## RHODES TOWN: TELEPHONE
## PREFIX 0241 POST CODE 85100
*Grand Hotel Astir Palace** (De Luxe)
1 Akti Miaouli
☎ 26284 (20 lines)

*Belvedere* (A)
PO Box 114
☎ 24471 (4 lines)

*Chevaliers Palace** (A)
3 Griva
☎ 22781 (25 lines)

*Mediterranean Hotel* (A)
35 Kos
☎ 24661 (5 lines)

*Park Hotel* (A)
12 Riga Fereou
☎ 24290

*Regina* (A)
20 Makariou
☎ 22171-2-3

*Riviera* (A)
2 Akti Miaoli
☎ 22581-2/24801

*Acandia** (B)
6 Iroon Polytechniou
☎ 22251-3/37774/37778

*Amphytrion* (B)
10 Alex Diakou
☎ 26880/26886

*Athena* (B)
G Leondos
☎ 22631-4

*Beach Hotel* (B)
19 Akti Kanari
☎ 23857

*Bella Vista** (B)
Akti Miaouli
☎ 29900

*Cactus** (B)
14 Kos
☎ 26100/26088

*Continental* (B)
8 Ag Ioannou
☎ 30885 / 30873

*Despo\** (B)
40 Vass Sofias
☎ 22571-2

*Esperia* (B)
7 Griva
☎ 23941-4

*Europa* (B)
28th October
☎ 24810 / 22711

*Manousos\** (B)
PO Box 92
☎ 22741-45

*Plaza\** (B)
7 Ierou Lochou
P O Box 246
☎ 22501-5

*Achillion\** (C)
14 Vass Pavlou Square
☎ 24604-5

*Adonis* (C)
7 G Papanikolaou
☎ 27791

*Als\** (C)
10 Vass Pavlou Square
☎ 22481-3

*Aphrodite* (C)
50 Othonos & Amalias
☎ 24668

*Diana* (C)
18 Griva
☎ 24677

*El Greco\** (C)
2 Georgiou Efstathiou
☎ 24071-2

*Florida\** (C)
5 Amarandou
☎ 22111 / 26843

*Hermes\** (C)
5 Plastira  ☎ 27677

*Isabella\** (C)
12 Amochostou  ☎ 22651-2

*Kipriotis* (C)
2 Valaoritou  ☎ 35921-5

*Lia\** (C)
66c Pythagora  ☎ 20371

*Lydia\** (C)
17 25th March ☎ 22871-2

*Marie Rodos* (C)
7 Kos
PO Box 214
☎ 30577 / 30583

*Petalouda\** (C)
49 Amochostou ☎ 24207

*Phaedra* (C)
7 Arcadiou ☎ 22791 / 24207

*Royal* (C)
50 Vass Sofias ☎ 24601-2

*Tilos\** (C)
46 Makariou ☎ 24591

*Vassilia\** (C)
55 Othonos & Amalias ☎ 24051

## Festivals

**Rhodes Flower Festival**
Every May.

## Tourist Information Centres

**Greek National Tourist
   Organisation**
5 Archbishop Makariou & Papagou
Streets, Rhodes, Greece.
☎ (0241) 23255 / 23655
Open: Monday to Friday 8am-2pm.

**Rhodes Town Information Office**
Rimini Square / Mandraki.
☎ (0241) 35945
Open (high season only): Monday
to Friday 9am-8pm, Saturday 9am-
2pm. Closed Sunday.

# Rhodes Town to Archangelos

**2**

If traffic is not too busy leaving Rhodes Town, around 40 minutes is all that is required to motor down to Archangelos. But with so much to see along the way 40 minutes could easily expand to a day or two or even more! Highlights include Koskinou, Kallithea Spa, Faliraki, Ladiko Bay, Afandou and its beach, Tsambika monastery, Tsambika beach, Epta Pigis (Seven Springs) and Stegna Bay. If time is running away, the options are to earmark some places for a return visit or to leave out Faliraki and Koskinou which can easily be visited by bus.

Leave Rhodes town following signs to Faliraki and Lindos. There are two routes out of town both signposted Faliraki, one following closely by the coast and the other taking a more inland route. Follow the inland route by turning right at the junction where Faliraki is indicated both to the right and straight on. The suburbs of Rhodes town have little to attract attention although this road passes Rodini Park on the right which once had deer but now just has peacocks to entertain visitors. Once through Asgourou, look for a signposted left turn to **Koskinou** which is located just after a short section of dual carriageway. Perched on the top of a steep escarpment, the village soon comes into view and is reached after 1 mile (2km). There is plenty of parking near the large church in the centre. Unfortunately, the church is usually locked so, unless there is a service in progress, it is not usually possible to look around.

Koskinou village is a maize of narrow, rambling streets crowded by traditional Rhodian homes with plant filled courtyards. The courtyards are mostly enclosed by large ornamental gateways, some very grand with arched doorways guarded by embedded ionic columns bearing an ornate entablature. It is one of only a few villages on the island which has made no concessions to tourism and has retained an old way of life. If you can find Yannis' taverna in the narrow streets, it is worth remembering the location. Only open in the evening, it serves excellent traditional Greek food and is well worth a return trip. Do not expect peppered steaks but if there is a party of four, try the *mezedes* and watch the table being filled with a whole range of Greek dishes and at very reasonable cost. Two people on their own simply end up with a smaller selection. But if its lunch time and food is beckoning, O Thanassi, has a good kitchen and you will have no trouble communicating with the Chef, she's Irish!

The expansion of Koskinou for tourist's needs has taken place 1½ miles (2½km) away down by the coast. Leave the village heading east to find it. It is mainly a collection of hotels and tavernas but there is a beach. On meeting the main coast road, turn left and very shortly right into the road signposted Eden Roc Hotel. A dirt road on the left leads down to the beach but it is best to leave the car at the top. It is a fair sized, sandy beach with limited water sports facilities. There is a further beach just to the south which has been taken over by the hotels. Although there are supposedly no private beaches on the island, once a hotel has furnished the beach with its own chairs and umbrellas there is often no space left and non-residents are not always welcomed. Attitudes do vary since some hotels invite the public to share their swimming pools and facilities to increase bar sales.

Return to the main road where self-caterers might decide to turn right to stock up at the large Miko supermarket just down the road; here prices are much keener than in the small supermarkets, otherwise turn left to head south.

Turn left to **Thermal Kallithea** (Thermai Kallithea), after 2½ miles (4km), opposite to a domed ruin on the right. The spa entrance is a little way down this road where there is a café-bar by the entrance and plenty of space for parking outside. There is no entrance fee for the spa.

This area has been famous for its spa water since antiquity but the present Moorish style buildings were constructed by the Italians around 1920. The lavish circular and domed buildings are set around a rocky inlet with a scattering of palm trees adding a touch of the exotic. Immediately through the entrance, a sad, dilapidated huge

*preceding page; Relaxing in the sun on Faliraki beach*

circular fountain sets the tone. Beyond, a grand Moorish arch, one of many, marks the entrance to a colonnade which leads down to the main spa building. The floor of the colonnade set with black and white pebbles is a fine example of the Rhodian art of *hochlaki* which is mostly seen in houses or courtyards. The black and white pebbles are set in patterns, sometimes geometric but often with floral or other motifs like the Byzantine eagle.

The circular domed building at the foot of the steps is where the waters were taken. Whatever ailments these waters cured, and they were good for the liver, the kidney and rheumatism, the effect on the bladder was dramatic judging by the number of toilets in the adjacent building. Simply follow the sign which indicates toilets. Only a few are now in use but walk around the circular building to see just how many there were. Outside there is a small beach which is used for sunbathing as are the rocks and pathway alongside the inlet where the mature palm trees act as sun umbrellas.

Return to the coast road and turn left for the 4 mile (6km) run to Faliraki. Very shortly the road closes with the coast and the whole sweep of **Faliraki** bay stretches out into the distance. The northern end of this beach is least attractive in sand quality and remains undeveloped although skeleton buildings now in decay which dot the route here tell of failed ambitions. Moments later the skeletal qualities vanish and the hotels are all large and flourishing. Although still 1 to 2 miles (2 to 3km) from Faliraki centre, this is hotel land where the great majority of the resort's hotels are situated. Those on the coastal side mostly have access to the beach behind. Where the hotels are replaced by shops and tavernas, Faliraki is close and when the junction is reached turn left down the main street and again at the roundabout near the beach to find a parking place.

Faliraki is a resort which tries to be all things to all people. If in search of activities, just about everything is there to be found, water sports in variety, water slides, go-kart racing, football competitions, bungee jumping or even snake watching at the snake farm; the list seems endless. Shoppers can shop to their heart's content from a touch of the exotic with eastern clothes from Bali Hai down to the standard tourist trivia. It is not too surprising that the criticism mostly uttered is that it is brash and noisy and it is, in parts. The main street, all tourist shops and supermarkets by day transforms at night. When the bars open it throbs with all the heat of a sore thumb. Every step down the road meets decibels of jungle beat reinforced here and there where the cacophony from nearby bars overlap. It takes a real artisan to know the music has actually changed! The youngsters love it and head there in droves during the evening. Trouble is not unknown and this is not the place to be for a woman on her own late at night. But this is only one short street and easily avoided if it is not to taste.

As always, there is another side and it is still possible to enjoy a more peaceful holiday. High density building is not a feature of the resort,

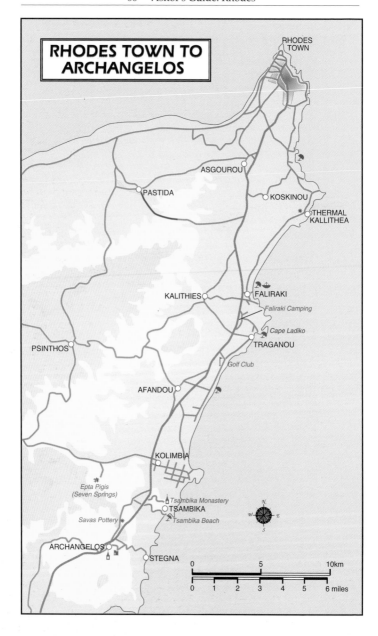

## RHODES TOWN TO ARCHANGELOS

RHODES TOWN

ASGOUROU

PASTIDA

KOSKINOU

THERMAL KALLITHEA

KALITHIES

FALIRAKI

Faliraki Camping

Cape Ladiko

TRAGANOU

PSINTHOS

Golf Club

AFANDOU

KOLIMBIA

Epta Pigis (Seven Springs)

Tsambika Monastery

TSAMBIKA

Savas Pottery

Tsambika Beach

ARCHANGELOS

STEGNA

0    5    10km

0  1  2  3  4  5  6 miles

*Koskinou is one of the few Rhodian villages which has not been affected by tourism*

*Thermal Kallithea spa, built by the Italians in the Moorish style*

quite the opposite. Faliraki covers a large area and, apart from hotel land on the northern edge, much of the accommodation is low rise rooms and apartments which are scattered around still with plenty of space between. It has also spread west of the main road in the direction of Kalithies. So there is quieter accommodation to be found and all the outlying areas are well served by tavernas. The beach remains the major feature and the resort attracts families. Good escapes from the crowds are found in the smaller bays at the south end of the resort where there are restaurants and tavernas overlooking the beach.

Eating in Faliraki is not always the pleasure it should be. The fare in most tavernas has moved away from traditional dishes to suit international tastes and, with a constantly changing customer base, trouble to do neither very well. Since Faliraki has few resident Greeks, they all live in nearby Kalithies, watching where the Greeks eat is no help. For good basic Greek food, Yannis' taverna O Kantas at the south part of the town near Hotel Colombia is worth seeking out. He serves his specialities, try his pork chops, to the Greeks in Kalithies village during the winter months but transfers to Faliraki for the summer. Some of the foreign owned restaurants are now serving the best food like the German restaurant Schweine Sepp and especially the English restaurant Partners at the foot of the Kalithies road. A good menu and excellent food makes it one of the most popular restaurants in town. Those who like to dine overlooking the sea might try Paradise taverna down the south end of the beach which also has a good reputation.

The main street is one way for traffic so return to the main road by continuing across the roundabout in a southerly direction then heading inland at the first opportunity. On reaching the main road by Asda supermarket turn left. If finding Asda is a surprise then Tesco, Sainsburys and Safeways too raise eyebrows but all these names have simply been hijacked and they have no connection to any major supermarket chain. Perhaps in a fit of pique at seeing all these names being snapped up, a nearby supermarket claims to try harder because they are not named after a famous English supermarket!

Once on the main road the Ladiko junction on the left is reached in a minute. Turn left here and keep ahead. The road passed on the right leads to Faliraki Camping, the only camp site on the island now that Lardos has closed. Stay left at the fork shortly reached to head down into **Ladiko** Bay. Here, headlands enclose a clear blue sea in a most intimate and picturesque manner. Little moves except for fishermen straightening their nets although tourist boats sometime anchor offshore to enjoy the swimming. Languid sunbathers using the facilities on the small sandy beach seem infected by the tranquillity moving only to the taverna at the rear when hunger or thirst demands it.

This is not the real Ladiko Bay, its just taken the name. The real bay of that name where the *Guns of Navarone* was filmed lies just to the north. The dirt track to the left 'on approaching' the beach leads to it and the short distance is manageable by car if taken slowly, although it is possibly more interesting to walk. Do not expect facilities in

Ladiko Bay, it has a rocky shoreline but it still attracts the sunbathers.

Return to the main road and continue south. **Afandou** Bay sweeping away to a backdrop of mountains is one of the islands most breathtaking views. Perspective presents the four individual and characteristic mountain peaks as a continuous range while in reality they are well separated in space. The inland peak guards Kolimbia junction, the flat-topped one to the left overlooks Archangelos and the two on the seaward side are on the headland at Tsambika.

Just 2 miles (3km) after joining the main road, turn left down by the golf course to reach Afandou beach. This 18-hole golf course is the only one on the island. The long, stretch of beach is mainly sand and pebbles edged by a sea of the most startling milky-blue. A slow enrichment of the beach is in hand as machines are used here to separate off the pebbles for aggregate while returning the sand to the beach. The military presence which restricted development seems now to have disappeared and holiday accommodation is slowly growing a little way back from the beach but for most of the time it is very quiet. Sunbeds and umbrellas are few but drinks and food are available from tavernas at the southern end. The masts and aerials at the extreme south end belong to a radio station which broadcasts the Voice of America.

Afandou is reached by taking the road from around the centre of the beach and driving inland, crossing above the main coastal road on the island's only flyover. It is a case of parking where you can in the centre. Afandou is the second largest village on the island after Ialysos. Apricots contribute towards its economy and hand made carpets once played a large part but less so now. Bustling about its daily business, the village seems to ignore tourism but there is an increasing amount of accommodation with all the dependent tavernas and services.

Return by the same road towards the flyover but this time filter right down the slip road just before to rejoin the main coastal road again heading south. There is a mere 2 miles (4km) to travel, hardly chance to relax and enjoy the scenery, before Kolimbia junction is reached and the road to Epta Pigis on the right. The tour in Chapter 7 also passes Epta Pigis so if time is pressing, it can be left out now and included later. Looking at the bare stony fields at the start of this road inland, it is hard to imagine that they are full of wild orchids in the early spring. The pink butterfly, *Orchis papilionacea*, is particularly common here. Open pine forest offers the first hint of verdancy before the junction for the **Epta Pigis** (Seven Springs) is reached after just 2 miles (3km). Turn left and head up to the car park. Alternatively, there is a pleasant woodland walk, about 10 minutes, from the junction which takes you to the heart of this beauty spot. Park here, if the coaches leave some space, enter the road for Epta Pigis but take the path on the right immediately and follow through the woodland.

The scent of pine on every breath, dappled sunlight, rustic bridges and trickling streams set the mood for Epta Pigis. Those who want to

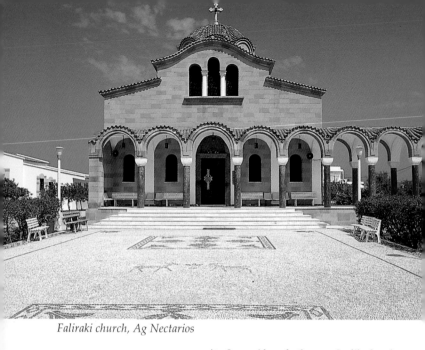

*Faliraki church, Ag Nectarios*

*opposite; Languid sunbathers on Ladiko beach*

*The azure-blue sea at Afandou beach*

rise to the challenge can wander at will around the maize of footpaths searching out the source of each of the seven springs. Lying across the entry road, a green lake nestles in a pine clad gorge. A signposted footpath leads to it from the main site as does a tunnel carrying a stream. Many people walk through the 610ft (186m) long dark tunnel but it can be dangerous when the water is racing or on emerging at the lake where it slopes steeply. Peacocks wander the site too and if they are not to be seen their penetrating cry is unlikely to pass unnoticed. Set in some of the deepest shade by the waters edge, the taverna is an atmospheric place to refresh and the food is good too. Before tourism, the Italians harnessed the waters of Epta Pigis to irrigate the orange groves around Kolimbia.

Return by the same route to Kolimbia junction on the main coastal road and cross directly over to head into **Kolimbia**. Once around the church, an avenue deeply shaded by mature eucalyptus trees runs straight as a die for 1 mile (2km) across the plain towards the sea. Park at the bottom.

Kolimbia, once all agriculture and fishing, is a rapidly developing purpose built resort constructed on the usual Greek scatter plan which may come together eventually. The avenue acts as the centre where most of the shops are to be found and around, mainly to the south, is an extravagantly laid out grid system of roads some still awaiting buildings. To the left from the end of the road lies a small fishing harbour with tavernas and beyond, accessible from an earlier track, is a good beach furnished with sun beds and umbrellas where some water sports are available. Boat excursions also leave from here. To the right is the fishermen's bay enclosed by a spit and beyond a taverna. A right turn just before the end of the road leads to another large sandy beach looked over by Tsambika Monastery. With an uncrowded feel, its an ideal place for a quiet beach holiday.

Turn left back at the main coast road to head for the next port of call, Tsambika Monastery. The road up to the monastery is just 1 mile (2km) further on and, although signposted (also Panoramic Restaurant), its narrow entrance is easily missed. This narrow concrete road winds steeply up the mountainside stopping short of the monastery in a small car parking area just beyond the taverna. There is still some distance to climb on foot but there is a good paved way to follow.

**Tsambika Monastery** is a tiny white Byzantine church perched high at 984ft (300m) with commanding coastal views both north over Kolimbia where the avenue of eucalyptus trees can be picked out and the grid layout appreciated and south over Tsambika beach and beyond to distant Lindos. Inside is the miraculous eleventh-century icon of the Blessed Virgin found on the mountain by a childless, infertile couple who later conceived a child. The legend is that if a childless woman wishing to conceive walks barefoot up the mountain to pray to the Virgin, she will be blessed with children. Children so inspired are named after the monastery, Tsambikos for a boy and Tsambika for a girl, a name unique to Rhodes. As it is so common on the island, it is more likely that fertile women named their offspring after the monastery by way of thanks that it had not been necessary to undergo this ritual. The saints day is 7 September, an especially potent occasion for the infertile.

**Tsambika** beach is easily reached by returning to the coastal road, heading south and taking the first left. There is plenty of space behind the beach for parking and even for a barbecue if organised. Enclosed by Tsambika's hill perched on the north side and a sandbank of a headland to the south, this beach of fine sand is as natural and inviting as they come. Facilities, although limited, are enough to ensure that a day can be lazed away beneath a sun umberella without having to stir too far for sustenance. There is just one eyesore to ignore, a tatty water slide which disgorges bodies into a frighteningly small concrete tank but at least there is not a hotel in sight.

On returning to the main road go directly across to join part of the old National road. It is only a 3 miles (4½km) stretch but a very scenic

# Savas Pottery

✳

Rhodes has a long history of pottery going back many centuries at least to the time of the ancient cities. The island has many keramic factories selling hand painted pottery, typically vases, plates and ash trays. Vivid colours, especially blue, feature strongly as do certain motifs which are uniquely Rhodian, the pomegranate flower and the stylised deer. Some factories also make copies of pottery found on the island's ancient sites but none better than Savas.

This family runs a true cottage industry. Outside on the potters wheel, Savas can sometimes be seen throwing pots or will demonstrate. Inside, his wife, usually assisted by their daughter, painstakingly hand paints the pottery with patience and admirable skill. Also outside is the brick built, wood fired kiln, primitive by modern standards but used to the same good effect. Firing the kiln, which is usually stacked full with many shelves of pots, is an art in itself. First the doorway is bricked up and the fire started with large pieces of wood. As the bottom of the kiln starts to warm, smaller pieces of wood are added to encourage the flames higher followed by finer pieces to ensure that the heat reaches the highest parts. Using the skills and experience passed down through the family, the uniform high temperature required for a successful firing is routinely achieved. Cooling is another low-tec highly skilled process. Bricks are taken out of the kiln walls at strategic points as required. The biscuit fired pottery which emerges is then ready for hand painting, predominantly in hues of orange and brown

Their speciality is replicas of ancient pottery found on the island and a seventh-century BC wine vessel or similar can be carried away at absolutely give-away prices.

run through olive groves. The first short section of road is rough but the surface is good again following the left turn at the T junction. It is up and away over the hills. The cluster of white buildings with a windmill on the descent is Savas Pottery. All the stages of pot making and painting can usually be seen here in a friendly atmosphere totally devoid of sales pressure.

On leaving the Savas Pottery, motor downhill to meet the main coast road, turn left and immediately right to head into Archangelos. Follow into the centre and park on the left immediately by the bridge over the river.

With 4,170 residents, **Archangelos** is one of the largest settlements on the island. At first sight, the modern centre sprawling beneath the medieval Crusader castle appears to have nothing to offer, apart from

*Every single piece is hand painted at Savas Pottery*

*opposite; The magnificent view south from Tsambika Monastery*

*A modern fresco of St George and the Dragon in the chapel of St George, Archangelos castle*

bars and tavernas, but the old town has plenty: white and ochre houses in narrow streets, brightly coloured gateways, blossoms trailing from painted cans, traditional houses and the wedding-cake white Church of Archangel Michael which gives the town its name. Thigh-length leather boots, snake protectors, which can be folded down in stages once filled the shoe shops. Snakes must be less of a problem as these boots are only made to order now but pairs are occasionally seen on display. Hand made carpets and ceramics are the town's specialities.

Wander ahead from the car into the main square and then left heading up towards the castle. Built by the Crusaders under Grand Master Orsini in 1467 as part of a chain of defences against the Turks (see the feature box on page 109) the outer walls are the only significant remains. Tucked away inside, occupying a corner position, is a little white church dedicated to St George. If the little old lady in black is around then its almost obligatory to step inside and admire the modern fresco of St George slaying the dragon. The icing sugar tower of the church is easily picked out from this vantage point, finding a route down to it through the maze of narrow streets is a different matter. It lies at the heart of the old town crowded in by houses. The wedding-cake style of church tower is commonly seen on this island and others in the Dodecanese group but this one at Archangelos is one of the prettiest. Cross vaulting, instead of the more usual barrel vault, is also a feature of church architecture on the island. Just outside the main entrance of the church, on the left when departing, there is a fine example of an old traditional house (see feature box on page 100). If the traditional old lady in black sitting outside offers an invitation, take it! It is too good to miss.

# Additional Information

## Places to Visit

**Thermal Kallithea**
Italianate spa
Open: every day, daylight hours, no admission charge.

**Epta Pigis**
Beauty spot
Open site, no admission charge.

**Faliraki**
*Snake Farm*
Reptile house
Open: every day, 11am-11pm.

**Savas Pottery**
Open: every day, daylight hours.

## Accommodation

**AFANDOU: TELEPHONE PREFIX 0241**
*Oasis Bungalows* (A)
☎ 51775

*Golden Days* (C)
☎ 61659

*Rose of Rhodes Apartments* (C)
☎ 22704

**ARCHANGELOS: TELEPHONE PREFIX 0244**
*Anagros Hotel* (C) ☎ 222480

*Anthi Sun* (C) ☎ 226190

*Caravos Hotel* (C) ☎ 229610

*Karyatides Hotel* (C) ☎ 229650

## FALIRAKI: TELEPHONE PREFIX 0241
*Apollo Beach Hotel* (A)
☎ 85535

*Calypso Hotel* (A)
☎ 85455

*Colossus Beach Hotel* (A)
☎ 85524

*Columbia Hotel* (A)
☎ 85610

*Rodos Beach Hotel* (A)
☎ 85471

*Erato Hotel* (B)
☎ 85414

*Mosses Hotel* (B)
☎ 85303

*Anasta Apartments* (C)
☎ 85311

*Diamantis Apartments* (C)
☎ 85236

*Hotel Evi* (C)
☎ 85586

*Gondola Hotel* (C)
☎ 85759

*Kostas Apartments* (C)
☎ 85520

*Telchinis Hotel* (C)
☎ 85380

## KOLIMBIA: TELEPHONE PREFIX 0241
*Irene Palace* (A)
☎ 51766

*Kolimbia Beach Hotel* (A)
☎ 51810

*Dounavis Hotel* (A)
☎ 56212

*Koala Hotel* (B)
☎ 56296

*Kolimbia Bay* (B)
☎ 56296

*Kolimbia Sky Hotel* (B)
☎ 56268

*Mistral Hotel* (B)
☎ 56346

*Relax Hotel* (B)
☎ 51320

## KOSKINOU: TELEPHONE PREFIX 0241
*Eden Roc Hotel* (A)
Kallithea Avenue
☎ 23581

*Sunwing Hotel* (A)
Kallithea Avenue
☎ 28600

*Kallithea Sun Hotel & Bungalows* (B)
Koskinou
☎ 62492

*Amazon Apartments* (C)
Kallithea Avenue
☎ 34523

## LADIKO: TELEPHONE PREFIX 0241
*Ladiko Bungalows* (A)
☎ 85536

## Festivals

Kalithies: dance festival in August.
Tsambika: Saint's Day 7 September.

## Transport

This area is well served with buses to and from Rhodes. See the Fact File for more details.

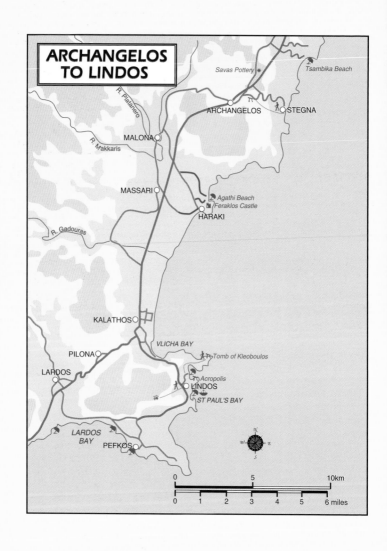

# ARCHANGELOS
# TO LINDOS

*Savas Pottery* ✳

*Tsambika Beach*

R. Platanero

ARCHANGELOS ○──○ STEGNA

MALONA ○

R. Makkaris

MASSARI ○

🏖 *Agathi Beach*
🏰 *Feraklos Castle*

HARAKI

R. Gadouras

KALATHOS ○

*VLICHA BAY*

PILONA ○

🏃 *Tomb of Kleoboulos*

LARDOS ○

🏛 *Acropolis*
LINDOS
*ST PAUL'S BAY*

*LARDOS BAY*

PEFKOS ○

N
W──E
S

| 0 | | | | | 5 | | | | | 10km |
|---|---|---|---|---|---|---|---|---|---|---|

| 0 | 1 | 2 | 3 | 4 | 5 | 6 miles |
|---|---|---|---|---|---|---|

# Archangelos to Lindos

The coastal region between Archangelos and Lindos is largely used for agriculture, especially so around Malona. Here citrus groves fill much of the countryside and the old National road which leads from Archangelos through Malona and Massari goes right through the heart of them. In April, with the scent of orange blossom on every breath, it is unthinkable not to use this route. The successful culture of oranges demands good summer irrigation and there is plenty of opportunity to judge the results in early season. Orange trees with either blossom or fruit on the trees all year round are never without interest but the harvest season is early, from January through to May depending on the variety. Farmers set up stalls alongside the main road and arrange colourful and eye-catching displays to attract trade from passing motorists. Neither Malona nor Massari have much to attract visitors except the ambience of a working Greek village. Old men relaxing in tavernas idly tormenting their worry beads while watching the tractors trundle through sort of atmosphere. In contrast to all the greenness of this area, Lindos is barren with barely any land for cultivation. Vines were grown there up to a few years ago but the wines they made were not of the best quality so they have now been rooted out.

If the diversion through Malona is not followed, use the good fast road from Archangelos to Lindos for a quick 12 mile (20km) run. There are a couple of side trips on the way, one to Stegna Bay and the other to Feraklos Castle, Agathi beach and Haraki, these last three lie close together. At the end of the journey awaits Lindos. With its white cubic houses clustered on the slopes below a fortified acropolis, Lindos is one of the most breathtaking sights in the Aegean. It is also one of those places which runs away with time. There is a case to argue for arriving early to beat the crowds. Just about every coach on the island visits every day but Monday, when the Acropolis is closed, although they seldom arrive before 9.30am. The disgorged tourists usually head up first to the Acropolis before doing the town then it's back to the coach and on to the next stop. The Acropolis opens early around, 8.30am, so there is a good hour for a leisurely inspection free of jostle. Monday is quieter with only the resident holidaymakers around and it is a good day to visit Lindos if the Acropolis is not on the agenda.

There is a good footpath through the countryside down to Stegna for those who prefer to walk, see the feature box on page 81. For car drivers it takes only a few moments. Follow the signposted road on the left just over the bridge from the parking place and fork left very shortly. The route is straight on at the next junction reached after ½ mile (1km) but note that the road joining from the left here is the intended return to the main road. Stegna is quickly reached. A stabilised track leads around the bay passing a selection of tavernas and giving glimpses of clusters of fishermen's cottages which are slowly being swamped by modern buildings. The beach is sandy shingle.

On leaving Stegna by the same route, take the first road off right and watch out for the small pottery on the left. Panayiotis specialises in undecorated terracotta with a good selection of large and small pots. Turn left on reaching the main coast road for the 4 miles (7km) journey down to the Haraki junction. Again turn left on a good road towards the coast. Ignore the first track off left signposted Agathi beach but take the second track which gives access to both Feraklos Castle and Agathi beach.

**Agathi** beach can be reached from the castle by following the track down. Skeletal buildings of an unfinished political development at the rear spoils the ambience but it does not detract when actually on the beach. Apart from excellent sand, do no t expect much in the way of facilities although this could change when a projected hotel complex is complete. Across the far side of the beach is the tiny Church of Ag Agathi built into a cave.

**Feraklos Castle**, another medieval castle, was actually used by pirates before the Knights of St John ousted them, reinforced the castle

*preceding page; An impressive view over Stegna bay towards Tsambika*

than used it as a prison. Reached from the track by a footpath leading to steps, it is a good climb and fairly rough underfoot. Make a mental note of the entry point into the castle since this is much less obvious on the return. Like many of these fortifications on the islands, the walls are the only significant remains. This one is no exception and the inside is overgrown with shrubs and other vegetation. Narrow footpaths lead around the enclosure and there are excellent views from the walls down to Agathi beach and to Haraki in the other direction.

Return along the track to the road and turn right to Haraki. Park just before the front behind the row of houses.

## Archangelos to Stegna Bay on Foot

Almost all of this walk is over stony footpaths through the countryside so that good footwear is essential. The return distance is around 5 miles (8km) so allow 1 hour each way. It is best to make a few mental notes on the outward leg since the return is by the same route or by the road if preferred.

Set out from the bridge in Archangelos initially following the road signposted to Stegna. Stay to the right at the fork reached in 2 minutes and turn left at the junction reached 3 minutes later to join a gravel track. There are small enclosed plots on your right for a time but 10 minutes into the walk take the small track forking off left. Olive groves set the scene, especially towards the end of the track approached 5 minutes later. Just before the end of this track follow a path forking left which skirts an olive grove and soon starts to descend to give views over Stegna Bay. Looking back from here there are good views of the old castle above Archangelos.

Very soon the path leads along the right edge of a gulley where the going becomes particularly stony and rocky but a slower pace allows more time to appreciate the fine scenery. No matter how dry and arid the ground here looks in summer, it is well decorated with flowers in early season, especially with the showy red turban buttercup, *Ranunculus asiaticus*. Once out of the gulley, the path leads around to the right above Stegna Bay. The route takes you south parallel with the bay and past it before dropping down to the coast. Follow the path to start with staying much the same height through the plots and olive groves. The path is not always clear since farm work destroys the line of the path in places but just keep making towards the white building ahead on the same level. Before reaching the building descend left on a path which passes to the left of a huge free standing boulder towards a concrete water trough. Go left on the descending track which leads into the bay.

*Enjoy the heritage and beaches of Lindos*

*A Lindian mansion with intricate cable patterning around the door*

*Orange seller on the Lindos road*

Separated from the main sweep of beach running south by a headland, **Haraki** nestles around its own intimate bay. Originally a small fishing hamlet, and the fishermen's cottages are still to be seen clustered near the headland, is has developed into a small settlement. A promenade divides the single ribbon of low rise houses, apartments and shops from the shingle beach. The exclusion of traffic adds tranquillity to the cosiness. It has a great atmosphere for eating and Stefanos' taverna on the front offers good Greek food but for something more upmarket Argo restaurant on the headland is the place, especially for fish.

Return to the main coastal road and turn south for the final run to Lindos. Kalathos comes first which always seems busier than its small size suggests, although its two filling stations may be the cause or even the luxurious Atrium Palace Hotel which is tucked away on the seaward side. It looks on to a sandy shingle beach which is steadily being enriched with the addition of more sand. This area was until recently in the hands of the military and generally out of bounds but is now starting to open up. Keep ahead at the Lardos junction or turn left for a quick diversion down to Vlicha Bay. This is another developing resort with two large hotels and some smaller ones looking on to a fairly good sandy beach. These are the nearest large hotels to Lindos.

Be prepared to stop almost on the first sight of **Lindos**. There is a view point with a large pull off on the left. From here the view is the inspiration of poets, painters and photographers. Golden sand edges

## Lindos: On Foot to an Inland Viewpoint

There is a short walk out of Lindos into the interior countryside leading up to a fine viewpoint which gives a wholly different perspective of Lindos. The impregnability of the huge monolith which bears the Acropolis can more readily be appreciated. Similar shaped rocks occur at Feraclos and Monolithos and both of those have been converted into strongholds.

Good shoes, at least trainers, are suggested since this walk is partly over stony ground. Allow around 1 hour for the return trip from the car park at the top of the hill.

From the car park follow south down the road towards Pefkos but only for a minute until the track before the new accommodation is reached on the right. Turn into the track and follow ahead, ignoring a track off left shortly, until the track bends around to the left. Before it bends left again, look for a strong path heading up the hillside to the right which is marked by stone cairns. Follow the path as it winds first up the bank and then through the field to reach a hillside. Carry on following the path until the crest of the hill is reached which is the viewpoint.

a violet limpid pool in the horseshoe bay, white houses are scattered in a dense ribbon on the hillside, each one snuggled against the next safely in the shadow and protection of the fortified Acropolis standing sentinel on the flat-topped hill above. It is a view which has persuaded more than one visitor that there can be no finer place on earth to live. Lawrence Durrell described Lindos as ' of a scrupulous Aegean order, and perfect of its kind'.

## The Lindian Archondiko

The Lindian mansion (*archondiko*) is unique to Lindos. Dress, customs, language and architecture all reflect this city's individuality evolving from a long history and commercial success over many centuries. From the beginning of the seventeenth century through to the nineteenth century, *archondika* were built from the wealth of ship owners and captains but the most grand and richly decorated were those of the early period. The architecture draws on elements from the Byzantine, medieval and Arab influences to create an individuality which is purely Lindian. Many of the early *archondika* are still in good condition and still occupied. Later mansions showed the more contemporary influences with the addition of a second storey and elements of neo-Classicism.

The best features in the island's own style of architecture was not ignored and central to the *archondiko* was a courtyard decorated with *hochlaki*, black and white sea pebbles with motifs sometimes reflecting the source of their wealth, fish and ships etc, or drawn from Byzantine art. Separated from the street by a high wall, a heavily decorated door (the *pylionas*) with an arched or horizontal lintel gave access to the courtyard. Around the sides of the courtyards, usually right and left of the *pylionas*, were the utility rooms, namely the kitchen, the oven, the stables, the toilet and maybe even a special room for an olive press. At the rear of the courtyard, opposite the *pylionas*, was the entertaining room, the *sala*, which was often the largest room in the house. The inner room was fitted with raised platforms for sleeping as described for the traditional house (page 100) except they were more lavishly decorated with carvings. All the inner floors were constructed with pebbles.

Another characteristic of the Lindian *archondiko* was the 'Captain's' room which can be traced back in prototype form to the time of the Knights of St John. This was usually located above the *pylionas*, or occasionally over the street and accessed by stairs from the courtyard. It was small compared with the *sala* but had many windows opening to the street, unlike the rest of the house. Outside, the façade and the door were richly decorated with cable patterns in relief and the lintel above the door usually bore a cross.

Parking can be a little problematic in midday. There is a large car parking area just where the left leads down into the town. There is usually space here since it means walking down into Lindos. There are lay-by's on the left, a little further down the road, which fill up early and further parking on the road to the beach and at the end of that road. Tourist traffic is not allowed in the main square at the bottom of the hill, except for turning and there is usually police traffic control directing everybody to the left along the beach road.

The square is as near to the village as traffic is allowed since the narrow streets were laid out long before the invention of motorised vehicles and more with the donkey in mind. Many of the houses in the village have been converted to tourist accommodation and moving luggage around is done by small three-wheeled pickups, probably converted from motorbikes, which chug along the narrow streets. Tourists arriving at night often have to part with their luggage in the main square and await its delivery the next morning! Lindos is under the protection of the Greek Archaeological Society which is concerned with the preservation of the village and only allows development which is totally in sympathy with the present structures. Despite these limitations, new developments are taking place expanding the village

*St Paul's church and the clear blue waters of St Paul's bay*

*The white-washed Byzantine church at Kalathos*

in the direction of St Paul's bay. Typically, white cubic rooms and apartments are built around a small courtyard with just one door opening to the street.

Even though Lindos is a magnet for tourism and the coaches pile in one after the other, the narrow streets soon absorb and disperse the crowds. Few day trippers have time to spare beyond the obligatory acropolis visit and a look at the beach. For them it is a quick tour and away. The main thoroughfares are covered for shade and colourfully decked with tourist trappings, T-shirts, carpets, post cards, and racks of souvenirs. Here also are the bars, tavernas and eateries of all description. Most of them tucked away well out of sight and some in the most delightful settings. Doorways open to courtyard cafés, like Gelo Blu recommended for its home made ice cream and excellent coffee, or up to roof garden restaurants. There is some good eating too in these smaller tavernas. Away from the main streets, the narrow side streets are also a delight to wander where turning every corner brings some new surprise. There are some finely sculptured doorways where an open door may just allow a glimpse into some flower-decked pebbled courtyard. In the heart of the village, just off the main square lies the domed Church of the Panagia. This fifteenth-century church has a dark interior with a black and white pebbled floor and is decorated with eighteenth-century frescoes by Gregori of Symi. With typical polarisation, male saints are on the right and female on the left.

Lindos sleeps at night only out of the tourist season. Bars and discos keep the beat going just as long as trading laws will allow and this changes more often than the bus timetable. If the noise at night raises complaints on the island then a closing hour of 12 midnight is imposed on the music, although night clubs are allowed later hours. Persistent cries of pain from the wallets of the bar owners are usually sufficient to restore late hours, until the cycle starts again.

In antiquity, Lindos is believed to have had a population of around 16, 000 compared to its present day 900. Before even the city of Rhodes was formed, Lindos was a powerful maritime trading post and it continued so into medieval times. The Knights of St John fortified the ancient acropolis to defend it against the troublesome Moslem forces. Lindos maintained its commercial power after the departure of the Knights by developing trading connections with Greece, Turkey and the Middle East. Buildings still remain from this sixteenth-century period of prosperity. Wealthy sea captains built some of the grander stone houses, *archondika* (see feature box on page 85) which were often typified by relief carvings of cable patterns around the doors and windows.

The way up to the Acropolis follows the main road from the square past where the donkeys are stabled. In 1961 it was estimated that there were 6,583 donkeys on the island, now there is probably not even 83 and most of those are here at Lindos! Gone are the days when a little old lady in black riding a donkey was found round every corner. Most visitors will leave the island without seeing a one. But the donkeys are here to carry visitors up to the Acropolis, at a price, of course. There is a choice and it is not too much trouble to make the ascent on your own feet. At least the donkeys are led on a longer and more gentle ascent and they do not mingle with the crowds. Going on foot, following the blue signs on the wall, takes you through the gauntlet of traders selling their wares and particularly the lace sellers who cover the embankment with their work on the final approach to the Acropolis.

Lace making and embroidery has traditionally been centred on Lindos since Byzantine times. Tablecloths and mats are the chief items on display and in such numbers that it is easy to suspect that the whole enterprise in now on an organised commercial basis.

There is a charge to enter the **Acropolis** on every day but Sunday. On Sunday sites of antiquity and museums are free throughout Greece to encourage Greeks to visit and enjoy their own history.

Once through the entrance and before ascending the long flight of **stairs** (1), there is a relief carving in the grey rock face depicting the stern of a ship in remarkable detail. A bronze statue of Agesandros of Lindos, honoured for his virtue and care of the people, once stood on the largest part of the ship. At the top of the rather steep **staircase** (1), the **castle** is entered through a vaulted chamber (2) which formed part of the Governor's Palace; the ruins of this extend to the north wall of the thirteenth-century **Byzantine Church of St John** (3) The Sanctuary of Athena Lindia occupies much of the plateau. At the extreme south end of the site stands the **temple dedicated to Athena** (4) which had solid sides with four columns to the front and the rear. To the north of the temple lies the once impressive entrance halls, the **propylaia** (5) and the **temple forecourt** (6). These formed three sides of a large rectangle and were complete with rooms and colonnaded passages. Below this to the north is the huge double-winged **stoa** (7) of which there are still many columns standing although most are obscured by scaffolding from the ongoing restoration. Below the stoa is a large terrace supported by a series of vaults and still further north, according to dedications on some of the statue bases which are scattered around, lay the small **Roman temple** (8).

A view over the north wall gives an oversight of the large harbour which was once busy with ships of the great Lindian fleet. At the end of the promontory which encloses the large harbour lies the tomb of Kleoboulos which can be reached on foot (see feature box on page 92). Assigning this burial tomb to Kleoboulos is apparently erroneous but the name still stands. Over the south wall the view is of the almost land locked bay where St Paul supposedly landed in AD58 and which is now named after him. It is known that St Paul did visit Rhodes on his way from Miletus to Syria to help convert the island to Christianity. Tucked away on the far side of St Paul's bay is the small chapel

# The Acropolis of Lindos

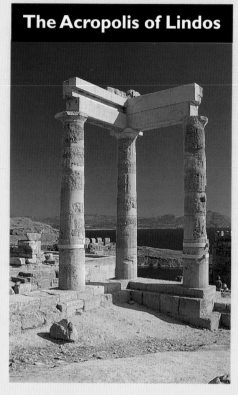

The enduring success of Lindos is almost directly attributable to a triangular flat-topped outcrop of rock, 380ft (116m) high, which juts out into the sea creating two natural harbours and presenting an easily defended stronghold. History traces occupation of this site back as far as the Neolithic Age (2500-2000BC) but, although findings suggest Mycenaean occupation, it was not until around the tenth-century BC that Lindos rose to great prominence along with the other two cities of antiquity on the island, Kamiros and Ialyssos. A temple dedicated to Athena Lindia has existed on this rock from at least this period.

Kleoboulos, who governed the city for 40 years in the sixth century BC, ruled moderately and wisely and drew great respect from all over Greece. He was included in the Seven Sages of Ancient Greece. By this time Lindos had become a great maritime trading city and had extended its trade zone to include Egypt, Cyprus and Syria. With the growing stature of the city, Kleoboulos improved the sanctuary to Athena by building a larger temple thought to have had a four columned portico at each end but without columns along the sides. The archaic staircase seen below the modern one may also be his contribution.

Shortly after the synoecism in 408BC, when the three ancient cities on the island decided to combine and form a new city, Rhodes, the Lindians modernised their temple along more Classical lines. A large entrance gateway, a propylaeum, was added giving the temple more majesty and a new staircase was built over the archaic one effectively to isolate the temple from the rest of the Acropolis.

Although Lindos lost some of its political importance after synoecism, its economic life was largely unaffected as was the fame of its sanctuary and it continued as a place of religious pilgrimage.

Around 342BC the temple built by Kleoboulos burnt down together with the statue of Athena and many of the votive offerings. The Lindians promptly built a new one in its place repeating the original style and built an even bigger statue showing Athena standing and not seated as in the original. The statue this time was built with a body of gold plated wood and limbs of marble. One of the most interesting finds from Lindos, made in 1904, is the Temple Chronicle now housed in the museum in Copenhagen. This was written by a local scholar, Timachidas, in 99BC and it describes many of the votive offerings of gold and silver by prominent historical figures of the day as well as some from mythical figures. One item on the list is the gift of a pair of bracelets from Helen of Troy. Other legends report that Helen of Troy gave a gold and silver vase made in the shape and form of her own breast by way of thanks since it was the sight of her breast that saved her from the wrath and revenge of Menelaus in Troy.

Later, in the Hellenistic Period around 200BC, further developments took place on the Acropolis which brought it to its final form. A huge double-winged covered colonnade, a stoa, was added on the north side embracing the steps up to the propylaeum and covering the whole width of the entrance. A small temple built in the north-west corner is thought to be Roman. On the western outer flank of the Acropolis is a fourth-century BC theatre cut into the rock with twenty-seven rows of seats still preserved. Also outside the Acropolis and near the theatre are the foundations of ancient walls believed to have formed part of a gymnasium.

The present fortifications are the work of the Knights of St John who, in the Byzantine era, re-modelled and strengthened the walls of an earlier fortification.

Excavations were conducted by a Danish team under Klinch and Blinkenburg between 1902 and 1914. There have been many studies since including one by another Dane, Einar Dyggve, in 1952. It was Dyggve who produced a reconstruction model which is still widely quoted. The Italians in their period of occupation of the island undertook some restoration work which has not proved as durable as the original.

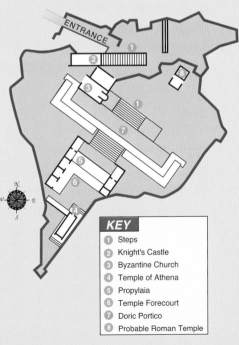

**KEY**

1. Steps
2. Knight's Castle
3. Byzantine Church
4. Temple of Athena
5. Propylaia
6. Temple Forecourt
7. Doric Portico
8. Probable Roman Temple

dedicated to him. Over the west, looking almost straight down, the ancient theatre can be seen cut into the rock of the hillside. From here too the flat-topped village houses which cluster around the sides and the base of the acropolis can be surveyed. The greenery which squeezes between the houses is a reflection on the number of courtyards which are far less obvious when down amongst the houses.

## On Foot to the Tomb of Kleoboulos

Good footwear, like trainers, are advisable as there is some scrambling up the rocks near the start which requires a little agility. Allow around 1 hour 15 minutes for the return trip. Leave Lindos town by the main beach road and follow it down to the beach, keep going until the café at the far end is reached. Head behind the café following the sign to the toilets and locate the steps cut into the rock. Climb these and follow a not too obvious path which leads upwards and to the right over the rocks. Once on top the path is more easily followed as it leads out towards the headland. A gulley holds up direct progress but once around this the way is clear to continue to the tomb. Looking over to right, Lindos can be viewed from a different perspective.

The large circular monument where the footpath ends is the Hellenistic Tomb of Kleoboulos. Built around the first century BC, several centuries after the death of Kleoboulos, it was sturdily constructed from rectangular blocks and fitted with a conical roof. Inside, the burial chamber was rectangular and the grave in the rock floor. At some time in its history it was converted into the Church of St Emilian.

With a good, deep stretch of fine sand, scenery second to none in the Aegean, an intimate feel in the enclosed bay and services immediately on hand, the beach at Lindos is an atmospheric place to be. Relaxing on a sun bed beneath a colourful umbrella, sipping a pina colada and gazing in awe at the curl of white sugar cubes around the Acropolis hill is great if you can stand the heat. The sun works overtime in Lindos and swirls its light and heat around the amphitheatrical bowl with an energy which creates even more heat. It is easily the hottest spot on the island and in summer temperatures frequently get as high as 49°C (120°F). The beach underneath the Acropolis is well supplied with tavernas and is often a little quieter than the main beach to which it is connected by a walkway.

It is easy to lose orientation walking through the narrow streets of the village which is the quickest way to get to St Paul's bay. The only advice is to try and keep the Acropolis to your left as you meander through the alleyways, although for much of the time the narrowness of the street blocks out the view. The route emerges by the flank of the Acropolis near a car park. For a close view of the theatre just follow up the side of the car park until the fenced enclosure is reached. Entry is not permitted but the perimeter fence allows a fairly close approach. Continue down the lane to reach St Paul's bay. This has a small shingle  beach which is used for sunbathing but there are very limited facilities. The chapel to St Paul is tucked away under the rocks on the far side. This side of Lindos is as yet undeveloped although new apartments in the traditional Lindian style are creeping ever closer to the bay.

# Additional Information

## Places to Visit

### Lindos
*Acropolis*
Open: every day except Monday, 8.30am-3pm.

## Accommodation

### HARAKI
There are no hotels but rooms and apartments are available.

### KALATHOS: TELEPHONE PREFIX 0244
*Atrium Palace* (Lux)
☎ 31601-2

### LINDOS: TELEPHONE PREFIX 0244
*Hotel Giota* (B)
☎ 42205

*Amphitheatre Apartments* (B)
☎ 31351

*Lindos Avra Apartments* (C)
☎ 31376

*Hotel Lindos Sun* (C)
☎ 31453

There are also many rooms and apartments in Lindos although most are taken up by tour operators especially in high season.

### VLICHA BAY: TELEPHONE PREFIX 0244
*Lindos Bay* (A)
☎ 42211-2

*Lindos Mare* (A)
☎ 31130

*Steps of Lindos* (A)
☎ 42249

## Transport

Buses ply the route between Lindos and Rhodes half hourly in the main season. The main villages, Archangelos and Afandou, are stopping points for all the buses but only some stop at the smaller villages. Vlicha Bay has no service at present.
Malona and Massari have in addition a separate timetable for buses into Rhodes.

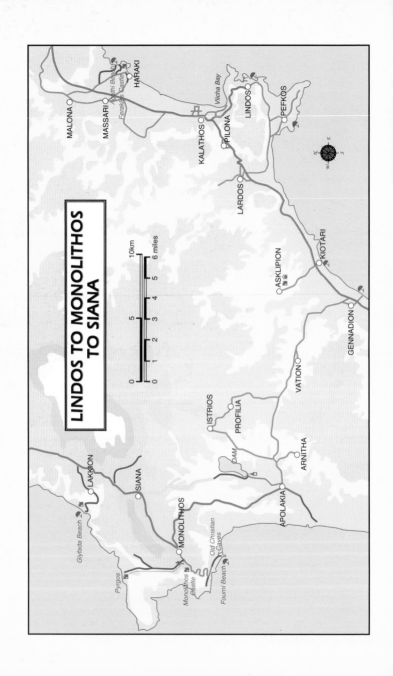

# LINDOS TO MONOLITHOS TO SIANA

10km

6 miles

Glyfada Beach
LAKKION
SIANA
Pyrgos
MONOLITHOS
Monolithos Castle
Old Christian Caves
Fourni Beach
APOLAKIA
DAM
ISTRIOS
PROFILIA
ARNITHA
VATION
ASKLIPION
GENNADION
KIOTARI
LARDOS
LINDOS
PILONA
KALATHOS
Vlicha Bay
PEFKOS
MALONA
MASSARI
Feraklos Castle
Agathi Beach
HARAKI

# Lindos to Monolithos to Siana

This tour looks at the southern part of the island using surfaced roads, from Gennadion via Vation to Apolakia, to cross over to the west coast. Pot holes are a danger on almost any road on the island but the stretch out of Gennadion tends to be poor. A good deal of annual road patching is carried out but winter just brings a new crop of holes.

Until a few years ago only the intrepid ventured beyond Lindos to explore the rural south and to discover the real Greek culture and people. All that is changing. Spurred on by the promise of a new international airport, developments have been taking place in villages like Pefkos and Gennadion and in coastal beauty spots where luxury hotels are springing into life. The airport remains a pipe dream but the hotels are reality. Holidaymakers gain a little and travellers lose a little. The old customs and culture are learning to adapt to the steady invasion and to serve a new master.

In this part of the south, the island is hilly rather than mountainous. It was, until 1987, richly cloaked in pine but no longer now the dim forests where saprophytic orchids once grew. In one of the island's worst natural disasters for years, fire ravaged virtually the whole of the south. Dead trees still scar the landscape. Left to its own devices, the cycle of nature plots its own certain course from destruction to regeneration. Taking advantage of the space and the light, broom has moved in to colonise the area and the hillsides now shine bright yellow throughout the spring. It will be future generations who see the forest eventually return. The whole area is very under populated, there are few villages and of these Lardos is by far the largest with a population of just 900.

Highlights along the route of this 37 mile (60km) journey include the emerging resort of Pefkos, Lardos, Asklipion, Gennadion, Apolakia including the nearby dam which is a good picnic spot, Monolithos with its crusader castle and, of course, the scenery.

Like a lady with that perfection of form, Lindos looks good from any angle. Taking the road out to the south gives yet another view which brings motorist to a halt for a last lingering look. Only from here is it easy to value the location of the old theatre cut into the rocky slope of the Acropolis. The left turn for Pefkos is a mere 2 miles (4km) and there is a short descent into the village. There is parking space by the first T junction.

**Pefkos** (Pefka, Pefki) is more of a happening than anything planned which possibly adds to its charm. The bits and pieces do not hang together just yet but they probably will some time. Perish the thought but Faliraki started as one street. There is one difference, the one street in Pefkos runs parallel to the coast and not towards it. The main beach is actually 5 or 6 minutes walk down a rather narrow access road. Although a sign indicates parking, there is still no conviction that this is the real world since there is only room for about two cars. The beach itself is good golden sand if on the narrow side while umbrellas and beds are on hand with tavernas not too far away. There is even a modern toilet block by the entrance to the beach but the locks for the doors have not arrived yet! Accommodation is sprouting up in a higgledy-piggledy way, fully in character with the resort. The main street has most of the tavernas and shops in town which probably means it can be called the centre. Addicts of Chinese food passing through might be disappointed to find the respected Shanghai Chinese Restaurant only open in the evening.

There is another beach to the west of the main beach which is a bit further away still, again with only a narrow access road. Fishermen's boats share this bay but beyond is a larger beach with access from the Lardos road. Pefkos is only a hop, skip and jump away from Lindos yet it might be a million miles. If peace and solitude top the list of holiday requirements then Pefkos fits the bill to perfection.

Leave Pefkos by the coastal road to rejoin shortly the road from Lindos. Eyes are needed for the road now for this too is another section

*preceding page; The splendid panorama surrounding the ruins of Monolithos Castle*

due for resurfacing. Lifeless Lardos bay looms on the left; another area inviting tourist development. **Lardos** village lies across the main coast road shortly reached. Head for the main square for signs of life and the cafés. Apart from the comings and goings of ordinary folk, there is nothing too much to delay visitors except perhaps Zorbas' Restaurant which offers an interesting menu including American as well as Greek dishes.

Back on the coastal road heading south, there is a glimpse of St George's beach with its umbrellas and painted taverna. It is a 6 mile (10km) run down to the Asklipion turn off but tiny Glystra beach snuggling into a crescent shaped cove is almost too inviting to pass without a closer look. Expectations of an invasion of unadulterated expansive Rhodian landscapes are dashed immediately around the short inland loop. Here high class Hotel Rodos Maris fills both sides of the road. With more imagination than usual, the architect has borrowed a little something from the past and introduced columns and porticoes to the neo-Classical to create an impression of a village evolved from antiquity. Only the seaward side is open for visitors, the development on the inland side awaits improvements on the cash flow situation. Almost next to it is another four star hotel, the Rodos Princess. Stretching out over a good distance, it gives the impression of single storey building but the fall away slope disguises a lower floor. It gives every room a sea view. Behind is a good beach which the hotel furnishes but it is doubtful if its guests actually leave the attractive outdoor pool area. Self-sufficiency is essential to survive this isolation and the Rodos Princess sees to every need providing excellent buffet style meals on a half board basis.

Around here is the home of the Rodos clay pigeon shooting club, the only one in Greece, and it is open to the public on payment of a temporary membership fee. Anyone interested in lining up a few clays through the sights of a 12-bore Italian Beretta should turn right opposite the Rodos Maris Hotel towards the Holiday Sun Hotel then follow the signs.

Turn right at the junction signposted Asklipion, head up into the village and park in the car park by the church.

**Asklipion**, watched over by a medieval castle, sprawls down the hillside without the benefit of a grand design but all the better for that. A traditional village in all senses it takes its name from Asklepius, the Greek god of medicine and Apollo's favourite son.

There is the story of tragic love mixed up here which ended up with the raven, previously white, being turned black. Apollo's lover Koronis while pregnant with Asclepius took another lover, a mere mortal. This news was carried to Apollo by a raven who was promptly turned black for her trouble. Still in something of a mood, Apollo killed Koronis and committed her body to the pyre but drew the child from her just before the flames struck. Asklepius later went off to learn medicine from Chiron, the centaur. The village here was once the island's healing centre with a hospital and doctors. Even now the sick still come but to seek healing at the church.

Like most small villages, it is alive in the morning with locals going about their daily routines. This is the time to see the bread makers in operation, to see folks out chatting and to see life in general. In the afternoon everybody sleeps. Siesta time is an undying tradition in Greece, summer or winter, and little moves between 2 and 5pm. Outside ovens are seen in many villages but here they are still regularly used. Blackened fronts and stored wood are the give- away signs but to see the bread makers in action rise with the lark. The village here is no stranger to tourism, but most of it, until recently, was

## The Bread Makers of Asklipion

Using the outside ovens for making bread is still practised by the old people of Asklipion. Bread is made just once a week in sufficient quantity to last the family until the next bake the following week. An early visit (9am) is essential to see this in progress. The ovens are pressed into more frequent use only on festive occasions and particularly at Easter time when vast quantities of *koulourakia lambriatika*, Easter biscuits, are made.

These outdoor ovens are fired up the previous evening using mostly pine wood and allowed to burn all night. There is no vent so the initial flames and the smoke issue out of the front opening which is eventually closed with a simple metal shutter. Overnight the fire burns to red

Greek tourism, drawn by the Byzantine church of the Dormition of the Blessed Virgin. Built in 1060, it started as a cross but extended later to accommodate a larger congregation. There are some fine frescos to see if the church is open, otherwise enquire at the taverna. Just next to the church is a museum displaying ancient religious artefacts, old bibles and ikons in the one room while the second room depicts the old way of village life with agricultural tools, bread making implements and even an old olive oil press. This is a co-operative venture by the villagers themselves who contributed many of the exhibits and well worth a few moments. Again, if it is closed ask at the nearby taverna.

Many of the houses in this village, as on the whole island, are simple

embers heating the stone floor and the walls very thoroughly.

Mixing the ingredients also starts the evening before allowing the dough to rise overnight. The shaped loaf, usually round, is stamped on top with a personal mark if the oven is shared with other users. The stamp is a wood carved roundel which may be hand made although commercial ones are available and sometimes seen in the older shops or in village hardware stores. Carefully wrapped in a tablecloth, placed on a board and covered again, the loaves are carried to the outside oven for baking.

Preparing the oven to receive the loaves is an important first step. Pushing the glowing embers to one side, the centre of the oven is thoroughly cleaned using a simple broom especially prepared on each occasion. Twigs of the evergreen mastic tree, *Pistacio lentiscus*, are tied to a wooden stave to make the broom. The mastic tree is one which has been used for centuries by the Greeks for medicinal reasons but chiefly for the fragrant gummy resin it yields. It is still grown commercially on the island of Chios where the gum is used in chewing gum, valued for preserving the gums and sweetening the breath, to flavour sweets, to make incense and, not least, in the manufacture of resins. Mastic is chosen for this use, not just because it is effective in brushing away the dust, but also for the clean fragrance it imparts which is believed to have antiseptic properties.

The loaves are transferred to the oven on a wooden spade and placed directly on the oven floor. When baking gets underway, the top of each loaf is brushed with water to give a good glaze. Another broom is used for this, one made from fresh sage twigs tied to a long stave, again to impart flavour. Any small piece of dough left over is usually made up into a small loaf which goes in the oven last and comes out first. Sometimes, a child or a tourist passing at the right moment might just receive the gift of a small loaf with the customary warning delivered by all mothers that eating hot bread makes you ill. A small sprig of fresh sage pushed through the bread allows the lucky recipient to carry away the hot loaf, and it tasted really good!

flat-roofed cubic structures without any redeeming architectural features. Inside is quite another matter. A number of the houses here are of the traditional Rhodian village style. The easiest way to see one is to find Sylvia's café which is located by walking ahead from the church car park through the next open space then bearing left. Sylvia is Greek Australian with good English and is happy to talk about life in the village.

 Above Asklipion broods the ruins of a medieval Crusader castle. It is a 15 minute walk to reach it following the broad track which starts

## Traditional Homes

The traditional village folk house, seen in Asklipion, Archangelos and Koskinou and many of the older villages on Rhodes, has only a single space inside. This simple style of house, seen also on other Dodecanese islands, has its roots in the era of the Knights of St John or more particularly in inheritance rights from that period. Here the first born daughter inherited the house and all her mother's possessions while the other children were expected to move out. Furthermore, it was a father's duty to provide a house for each of his daughters as a dowry. This basic, simple structure, intended to house a complete family, parents and children, provided the most economical solution.

Apart from the doorway, there may be no other opening or perhaps a window in the front wall. Inside, a wide archway indicates a division between the living section and the sleeping quarters with the floor usually set with black and white pebbles. Peripheral benches and raised platforms provided the furnishing leaving the central area clear. The fireplace occupied a corner by the front door. The matrimonial bed was a raised platform about 5ft (1½) high which was enclosed by an embroidered curtain, a *sperveri*. The children also slept on a platform, normally slightly lower, either close by or on the opposite wall. By the fireplace was the *soufas*, a low platform upholstered with carpets or mattresses for sitting and dining. *Soufas*, like the English word sofa, probably derived from the Arabic *suffah*. Storage cupboards for bedding and linen and for oil, wine and food were arranged under the high platforms. Benches completed the furnishing which also served for storage.

Embroideries, fabrics, plates and pitchers were all used as interior decoration, especially plates. Decorative plates were especially important and would cover the whole side of the wall facing the door relieved only by a mirror. Often the plates were sent home by migrant family and a vast number indicated a form of wealth.

just to the right of the toilets. After an impressive entrance, there is little to see inside the castle except for good views over the countryside but care needs to be taken for uncovered wells. As the story goes, there was at one time a tunnel from one of the houses to the castle so that villagers could secretly gain refuge from raiding pirates.

Leave Asklipion back to the coast road and cross directly over to reach the beach and the area known as **Kiotari**. This was the site of the original village of Asklipion but it was forced inland by piracy probably in the period from the seventh to the nineth century. Piracy at this time was particularly troublesome to the islanders and many old settlements were destroyed or driven inland. Fortifications too were built and it is from this time that the castle at Asklipion may have its origins.

The land by the coast here belongs to the church and the villagers are allowed to build simple beach huts which they use in summer. A section of the old national road, not all of it with a hard surface, runs both north and south along the coast. Moles and sand-spits divide up the shoreline into smaller bays, some sandy, others strewn with seaweed disguised as wood shavings. Shaded by tamarisk trees and lapped by an ever-blue sea, it contrives to be picturesque in a way not seen elsewhere on Rhodes. Just to the south lies the Lighthouse Restaurant which looks interesting.

Running southwards, Kiotari beach blends seamlessly with  Gennadion's beach. It is risking a bumpy ride to follow the old unsurfaced National road so, for comforts sake, it is easier to return to the main coastal route. If another good reason is needed then its provided by Angelaki's snack bar on the right before Gennadion junction. Although small, snack bar is a misnomer since full meals are also served and good Greek food is available at yesterday's prices but it pays to brush up on the Greek first! Ignore the turn off right to Apolakia which will be the onward route shortly but first take a look at the coast by turning next left. A colourful rash of sun shades in orderly rank is as unexpected as rain in August this far down south but this shingle beach is the playground of fast growing **Gennadion**. Located inland of the main road, Gennadion has seen steady tourist development over the past few years outgrowing its tag of 'sleepy hamlet'. Wander at will and try to find the Italian built police station but without a recognisable centre it is hard to know where to start and finish. Not so difficult to find are modern supermarkets and tavernas which are scattered around but the place only really comes to life at night when people return from the beach.

Leave Gennadion by taking the road out to Apolakia and hope the pothole fixers have visited the early part of the road. Flashes of electric blue skimming around the fields here are likely to be bee-eaters, especially if their soft liquid chrrup call is also heard. They tend to congregate on the telephone wires along the roadside so keep the binoculars handy. Apiary is common in the south, but the beekeepers

*Siana*

*The early Christian caves at Fourni*

can hardly be pleased to be supporting such a good population of bee-eaters. The surrounding low, rolling, scrub covered hills, lively and colourful in spring retire drab and listless in summer, but scent the air with heady aromatic odours of rosemary and thyme.

On entering Apolakia, watch out for the road off right signposted 'Dam'. It is a 2 mile (4km) diversion along a surfaced road to reach a ✳ viewpoint over the artificial lake. Normally very peaceful, it is an ideal place to picnic and unwind from driving. Even this lake assumes the Aegean blue of the sea and beyond, on a distant hillside, the white houses of Siana cluster below the peak. The road continues from the dam as a track all the way up to Siana. For those with itchy feet, it is around 9 miles (14km) for the return walk. To the side of the dam lies the little white church of Ag Theotokou.

**Apolakia** exists around a major junction and is a great watering hole. It only seems to come to life with the arrival of the daily bus. The wise elders drink coffee in the *kafeneon* while everybody else is out in the field busy growing melons. It is very much an agricultural town which sees only a passing tourist trade. Once through, turn north for the 7 mile (11km) run to Monolithos. It is a gradual rise towards the Akramitis mountains along a meandering route through forested countryside. On the eastern side of the island, the rolling hills descend gently towards the coast leaving some coastal plain. Here on the west coast, more particularly from Monolithos northwards to Skala Kamiros, the mountain crowds in on the sea and the road is often forced to a higher level.

**Monolithos** village slumbers at the foot of Akramitis and is little disturbed even when the coaches thunder through en route to Monolithos castle which is firmly on the tourist agenda. The road runs 🏰 alongside the village so, unless an effort is made to get out and walk around, little is seen of the way of life there. Most of the tavernas too are located on the through route to catch the passing trade, especially coach parties. The road down to the castle is good but drive slowly so the view point from above is not missed. Monolithos castle sits astride Monopetra, a blunted needle of grey rock rising precipitously to 774ft (236m). This is no fairy tale castle, but a real life impregnable fortress built by the Grand Master d'Aubusson. The thick walls thread around the top and inside is the white church of Ag Panteleimon. Steps lead 🛉 up from the car park below the castle to an area enclosed by the walls. From the top the views are absorbing both along the coastline and of the offshore islands including Halki.

Following the coast road for 2 miles (4km) after leaving the castle leads down to Fourni. The road is surfaced part way but eventually runs into track which is comfortable to drive if taken slowly. There is a small beach of sandy shingle at **Fourni** with no facilities except for a canteen in high season. It is not the beach but the early Christian caves which provide the interest here. To reach them, cross the beach heading for the base of the spit of white rock at the far end. Follow the narrow path to wind up and round onto the top of this. The caves are well concealed on the southern face and there are steps which lead down to them, although they are not especially easy to locate. Be warned, these old, badly worn steps are close to the edge and dangerous. Despite this, people still go down! The caves date back as far as the seventh century when Christians went into hiding to escape persecution from first the Persians and then the Arabs.

# Pyrgos on Foot

There is nothing at Pygos except the *pyrgos*, a watch tower, and a long since deserted settlement. Problems in the defence of the long stretch of hostile coastline north from here were solved by castles at Monolithos and Kritinia with a chain of watch towers between. The tower at Pyrgos is particularly well preserved and this walk provides one of the very few opportunities for a close look. There is another one to see at Glyfada beach, but not in such good condition, for those who follow the side trip described in the following chapter.

This walk takes place over tracks which are generally comfortable underfoot but stout shoes or trainers are strongly recommended. It is downhill all the way and uphill on the return. The distance is 7 miles (12km) for the round trip and it requires about 2½ hours walking time in addition to time spent at the site which makes a full half day excursion. To find the start of the walk, drive out of Monolithos on the castle road and look for the track on the right, in just over ½ mile (1km). It is identified by a sign for Kimisala and a battered no entry road sign. Park here and set off on foot down this track which leads at first along a contour of Mount Akramitis on the seaward side. There are fairly open views in the early part of the walk. Stay left in just over half an hour, where the main track forks around to the right, and descend into the shade of the pine trees. Eventually, after a steady descent ignoring tracks off left, when the sea more or less comes into view, the way divides. To the left leads to the tower on the coast while to the right is the remains of an old settlement. The path down to the *pyrgos* provides a good overview of the old settlement. Return by the same route.

Return back along the same road towards the castle then the town of Monolithos and continue northwards to Siana. Wending through pine alongside Akramitis, the scenery takes on a mountainous aspect with glimpses of the stark, barren summit of Ataviros, the highest peak on the island. **Siana** arrives quickly enough and there is usually space to park near the church. Like a number of hinterland villages on Rhodes, it is built on a hillside and is best seen on foot. Looking south, the dam visited in the earlier part of this tour can be clearly seen. Siana is famous for its honey and its *suma*. Four kinds of honey are made, according to the season: flower honey from the pollen of spring flowers is made in April and May, thyme honey in June and July, pine honey in September and October and heather honey in December. *Suma* is a strong spirit made illegally in other parts of the island but, by a quirk of history, is legally made under licence here. Anyone looking to try a sample of this local firewater should pop into Steve's taverna.

## Suma and Ouzo

Wine has a by-product in the form of grape skins, seeds, pulp and stems, known collectively as *raki*, which can be distilled to produce a strong spirit. Subtle flavours are introduced by the infusion of certain herbs, like fennel or aniseed, before distillation and all these products were originally called *raki*. *Ouzo* has grown out of this process. No longer is it made from the wine residues but from pure alcohol made from molasses with the addition of aniseed. Well made *ouzo* contains around 46 per cent alcohol and is usually taken with ice or water. Dilution with water liberates the aromatic oil anethole, introduced from the aniseed, to turn the drink milky, sometimes more so or less so depending on the actual manufacture. Generally, dense cloudiness indicates high quality. To the casual drinker, all *ouzos* taste much the same but the various brand names have different followings, some achieving wider recognition throughout the country than others. For the Greeks, *ouzo* is more than just a drink, it is blue sky, warm air, sunshine and even more, it is the breath of the soul, a drink to share for male bonding. Traditionally, it must be taken with a little food, with nuts or *mezedes*. *Mezedes* is a small plate of food, typically a few small bite size pieces of bread, some olives, a bit of cheese, a meat ball or anything that the taverna is cooking that day. Now it is usually a few nuts but in some of the older villages *ouzo* is still served with *mezedes*.

*Suma* is the product of distillation of the wine residues without any additions. It is made almost everywhere that wine is made although it has different names on different islands and in different parts of the country. Here on Rhodes it is *suma*, on the mainland, particularly the north, *tsipouro* and on Crete *tsikoudia*. Much of it is made illegally but here in Siana some farmers were granted a license by the Italians which was never rescinded and is still recognised by the present authorities. Mostly, it is not possible to buy *suma* to sample or take away because it is usually illegally made but here in Siana, at Steve's taverna, you can do both of these.

# Additional Information

## Places to Visit

### Asklipion
*Museum*
Open: on request. Small admission Charge.

### Monolithos
*Castle*
Open site. No admission charge.

## Accommodation

### ASKLIPION: TELEPHONE PREFIX 0244
*Hotel Rodos Maris* (A)
Kiotari, Asklipion
☎ 430000

*Hotel Rodos Princess* (A)
Kiotari, Asklipion
☎ 43102

*Hotel Holiday Sun* (B)
Asklipion
☎ 44133

*Kiotari Beach* (C)
Kiotari, Asklipion
☎ 43321

*Kanbanaris Bay Hotel* (C)
Kiotari, Asklipion
☎ 43279

*Villa Sylvana Apartments* (C)
Asklipion
☎ 44116

### GENNADION: TELEPHONE PREFIX 0244
*Christiana Apartments* (C)
☎ 43228

*Betty Apartments* (C)
☎ 43020

*Hotel Dolphin* (C)
☎ 41084

*Hotel Evangelos* (C)
☎ 43329

*Gennadi Sun Apartments* (C)
☎ 43057

*Golden Sunrise Hotel* (C)
☎ 43003

*Olympos Apartments* (C)
☎ 43256

### LARDOS: TELEPHONE PREFIX 0244
*Hotel Nenetos* (B)
☎ 44209

*Hotel Sunshine* (B)
☎ 44128

*Hotel Lardos Sun Beach* (C)
☎ 44203

*Hotel Lostas* (C)
☎ 44271

*Smara Apartments* (C)
☎ 44264

*Zinovia Apartments* (C)
☎ 21867

### MONOLITHOS
*Thomas Hotel* (B)
☎ 0241 85403

### PEFKOS: TELEPHONE PREFIX 0244
*Pefkos Beach Hotel & Apartments* (C)
Pefkos, Lindos
☎ 44431

*Hotel Thalia* (C)
Pefkos, Lindos
☎ 44458

*Hotel Summer Memories* (C)
Pefkos, Lindos

# Siana back to Rhodes Town

# 5

Throughout history the western coast below Kamiros has never attracted settlements of any great size or number. Poor access to the sea, a hostile physical geography, poor land quality for agriculture or livestock and even unsuitable climatic factors are all deterrents. With a fairly constant westerly wind, and some altitude above the sea, this region is distinctly cooler in summer and probably cold in winter. It is this cooler micro climate as well as edaphic factors which now supports the island's most successful region of viniculture centred near Embonas. Piracy too remained a problem, especially from the seventh to the ninth centuries, and where tempting cultivable land lay on the slopes in view of the sea, temporary summer farm settlements developed. Lakkion, visited shortly is one such settlement which still farms in the same way even today. Defending the coastline too was problematic but solved by having castles at Monolithos and Kritinia and a chain of watch towers, *pyrgoi*, on the coastal areas between. One of these near Monolithos is featured in a walk, (see page 104) and another on the side trip down to Glyfada Beach described shortly. In the time of the Knights of St John, these towers were constantly manned and in times of danger signalled by either primitive semaphore or pigeon by day and beacon fires by night to ensure that the alarm was passed from fortress to fortress.

North of Kamiros, the mountains progressively fall away and the amount of cultivable land increases as does the number of settlements. Closer still to Rhodes Town, especially from the airport northwards, is some of the densest development on the island and much of it for tourism. Why this area in particular has seen such development is hard to appreciate. Certainly it is convenient for both Rhodes Town and the airport but the beaches, mostly narrow, usually shingle and sometimes non-existent, in no way match those of the east coast. It is a very windy part of the island too although this comes as something of a blessing in the heat of high summer. Almost as a compensation, the accommodation offered in this area is amongst the finest on the island and it has a near monopoly of luxury class hotels. The Rodos Palace, for example, describes itself as a resort hotel offering, apart from both indoor and outdoor swimming pools, a range of facilities second to none from bars to beauty salons, from satellite television to shopping arcades as well as a French restaurant, La Rotisserie, which provides some of the best eating on the island. With a large lecture theatre to seat 1,000 and smaller ones beside, the hotel also has outstanding conference facilities and hosted the E.C. summit meeting in December 1988.

Wild and rugged scenery in the early part of this tour gives way to coastal plains and cultivation but there are plenty of highlights along the way; Kritinia and its castle, the ancient city of Kamiros, another ancient site, Filerimos, and the resort areas of Trianda and Ixia. Monday is not a good day to see the ancient cities, they are both closed. On the other hand, Sunday is a good day since entrance is free.

Leaving Siana northwards, the road continues at high level with the stark grey mass of Mount Ataviros exerting an even greater presence on the right. By contrast, the offshore islands over left of Alimnia, Tragoussa, Strongili and Makri have an ethereal quality, floating in a blueness of uncertainty where sea and sky merge to banish the horizon. Scene gazing or not, once beyond the Ag Isidoros road, watch out for the left turn down to **Glyfada** beach. Despite its name, it has no beach. What it does have is two tavernas, one of them right on the shoreline, and with no passing traffic they are really atmospheric places to eat. Unfortunately, the road down, which starts with a hard surface, is track which is a slow drive for the 7miles (12km) round trip. Part way down is a view of Lakkion, partly deserted but still used as it always has been for summer farming. Captain Gregoris' fish taverna, with rooms to let, is first encountered but follow right along the seashore to reach Paradise fish taverna. Next to this is the remains of an old watch tower, a *pyrgos*.

*preceding page; Sun umbrellas on Trianda beach, angled against the constant breeze*

# Fortresses and Castles on Rhodes

As a result of intense pirate activity in the seventh to ninth centuries AD and the activities of the Knights of St John, the island has a remarkable number of castles and fortresses of which many have survived. The seven principal ones are at Rhodes Town, Archangelos, Feraklos, Lindos, Asklipion, Monolithos and Kritinia all of which are visited in the appropriate chapter.

Defence against the infidel Moslems was an ongoing concern of the Knights which spurred them into almost constant building and reinforcing. Twelve fortresses were known to exist under Grand Master E.B. Degli Orsini in 1479 which had to serve 44 settlements but the full total was thought to be around 16. Each settlement was instructed on evacuation procedures and assigned to the various castles. Settlements at Gennadion, Kalathos and Lardos were assigned to Lindos castle for example. Other castles mentioned in these instructions were located at Apolakia, Lahania, Katavia, Apollonia, Salakos, Fanai and Villanova as well as the fortifications at Filerimos. In addition to these, there are castle remains found at Lardos and Mesanagros. Towers, *pyrgoi*, were also built around coastal regions, especially on the west coast as an integral part of the elaborate defences. Some of these are still in good condition, especially the one at Pyrgos which is visited on foot in Chapter 4.

Most of the roads leading off the main road in this section seem to arrive with minimum announcement and are easy to miss. This is true of the left fork leading into **Kritinia**. The modern road detours quite circuitously around the village with a link road from either end. Take the narrow left fork down through the village and park where you can, perhaps past the main church. Here is a village which, although on a slope, for once does not straggle down the hillside. Not too far from the sea, the location is, nevertheless, hidden but within sight of the castle. Thought to be settled by immigrants from Crete (Kriti), Kritinia has something almost unique on the island but common elsewhere in Greece, a true village square, a *platia*. This is located below the church giving commanding views down towards the castle. Two tavernas compete for custom but whichever, with plenty of colour from the surrounding floral display, it is a relaxing atmosphere to sit and watch the world go by. The village has a small folk museum but this is located  in the imposing building outside the village on the main road heading north. Local costumes and farming implements are amongst the exhibits as too is a tripod cradle which held baby while mother worked the land and hollow gourds used not just to carry water but also to

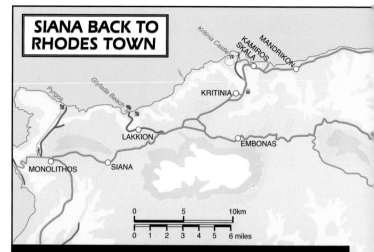

## SIANA BACK TO RHODES TOWN

# A Castle Circular On Foot

Below, but out of sight of the castle, a gorge cuts through the hills to the sea. From the coastal end of this gorge, a fairly short but uphill footpath returns to the castle completing an attractive circular walk. The complete walk takes around 1 hour and, while some of it is over tracks, much is over stony footpaths which for comfort and safety demand good footwear.

Follow the track down from the castle entrance and turn right at the first junction. Keep ahead to the T junction and turn left to join another track. Soon, after just a few minutes, notice the water pipe starting on the right and turn right onto a lesser track still following the direction of the water pipe. About 3 minutes along here, when another track is encountered on a bend, turn left to meet very shortly a more obvious track which is followed down to the right. Now heading toward the sea, watch out for the point where the track reduces and starts to descend to a streambed. Fork right here onto a clear path which rises a little and heads off around the hillside. The deep ravine falls away on the left but the path stays at a high level for a time giving spectacular views then descends gradually to the seashore. Stay close to the right hillside and look for the path from the shore that ascends the hill back more directly towards the castle. This well defined path leads in winding ascent to emerge in a field. Cross this to join the track and turn left towards the castle. Ignore the first track left but take the second to return to the castle and complete the circuit.

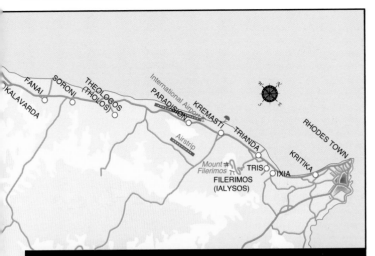

*The gorge used in the circular walk from Kritinia Castle*

keep it cool. Only small but well worth a stop. The panoramic views from the café terrace here are very persuasive

In sight from here, the castle is the next port of call so watch for the narrow road off left signposted for the castle. It is a bumpy ride over one short section which needs to be taken slowly. Just before the entrance to the castle, one of the local ladies usually leaps out with a notice which explains that she is in charge of the castle and solely responsible for its upkeep and maintenance. While there is no charge for entrance, the notice explains, it would help if some of her fruit or vegetables were purchased! To lend authority to this, her Greek identity card is usually proffered. This clever local enterprise usually works because the produce looks so fresh and the lovely old dear so inoffensive! Still, it is a long time since the castle has been swept out.

Perched on a rock (430ft/131m), it is not too much of a climb to enter the castle. This is another built by the Knights of St John originally on three levels with each level assigned to a different Grand Master. Apart from remnants of the chapel, there is little to see of internal structures but it is interesting to wander around.

It is a much smoother ride returning northwards from the castle to the main road since this section is surfaced. Almost immediately on rejoining the main road, be prepared to turn left into **Kamiros Skala** which is nothing more than a small harbour and a handful of tavernas. This was the port of ancient Kamiros but possibly too far away to have developed significantly.

The boat to and from Halki docks here, arriving from Halki in the morning and returning at 2.30pm Monday to Saturday. A bus from Rhodes Town serves both the arriving and departing boats. To spend a day on Halki midweek requires a two night stopover, unless a few hours is enough with one night there and a 6am return. Sunday is different. A day trip runs Sunday departing Kamiros Skala 9am promptly and Halki at 4pm. At the moment there are no buses on a Sunday from Rhodes Town. See Chapter 10 for further details on Halki.

Kamiros Skala is the place for fresh fish and the tavernas here are known throughout the island. Unfortunately, the tour parties know it too so lunchtimes can get crowded. Apart from the coach parties, it is a fairly sleepy place unless a fish catch is being landed or the Halki boat is around.

With the mountains left behind and down again at sea level, agriculture takes over. A sea of plastic greenhouses and an impressive church is **Mandrikon**. Continuing north, picturesque seascapes come and go as the road follows the coastline towards Ancient Kamiros. Turn right for the short diversion to the ancient city and park in the area outside the gates.

**Kamiros** was one of the three ancient cities on the island. First settled by the Mycenaeans, it was later colonised by Dorians around

1100BC. It grew steadily in prosperity keeping apace with the other Dorian cities of Ialysos and Lindos but only until the synoecism of 408BC leading to the formation of a new city, Rhodes. Kamiros went into decline but continued to be inhabited into the early centuries of Christianity until, at some time around this period, it was finally abandoned. The hills surrounding the ancient city are full of cemeteries which have proved of enormous interest to the archaeologists and yielded many fine pieces now housed in the museum in Rhodes Town, including the grave stele of Kroto and Tamarista.

The old city was built on a hollow slope of a hillside facing northwards. The residential part of the town occupied the lower slopes while the acropolis, including the religious and public buildings, sat on the top of the hill behind. Unlike the other two cities, Ialysos and Lindos, it was not fortified. After centuries in oblivion, it was rediscovered in 1859 and excavated by Biliotti and Salzman and further excavated by the Italians from 1929 onwards. Revealed now is a ground plan of houses, streets and sanctuaries covering an extensive area and representing the finest example in Greece of the residential sector of an ancient city.

The entrance leads into a **sanctuary** with a fountain (1). To the north of this, and first encountered, lie the remains of a **Doric temple** of unknown dedication (3). Further east is the **Sanctuary of the Altars** (7) which was a sacrificial area with nine alters, including a large one, and all still in good condition. Running uphill to the south is the main street which gives a close view of the remains of the domestic dwellings. On the left, higher up, are the remains of a **private house** with part of the colonnade restored (8). Parts of the sophisticated drainage system are visible at the top of the street.

On the highest point is a **sixth-century BC cistern** (10) and behind, a huge third-century BC **stoa** fully 656ft (200m) long with two rows of Doric columns (9). There were rooms behind the columns which were probably hotel rooms for worshippers visiting the temple. The **temple** of **Athena Kamiros** (12) lay behind and only parts of the foundations now remain. From the stoa there is an excellent overview of the old city.

Retrace the route down to the coast road to continue northwards. If refreshments are in order, or if its time for a meal, there is a taverna Akroyiali with a delightful ambience down on the coast shortly after rejoining the main road. It looks on to a quiet stretch of beach where the fishermen, if not landing a catch, are kept busy sorting out their nets. There are more than a few places on the island which combine good food with a good atmosphere.

It seems reasonable to expect that the coast road is the major route so to give way at the Kalavarda junction comes as a surprise. Watch out once through Fanai for the long single lane bridge. Tourism is slowly creeping down this coast although it almost seems without reason.

*Kritinia Castle*          *opposite; The sanctuary at Ancient Kamiros*

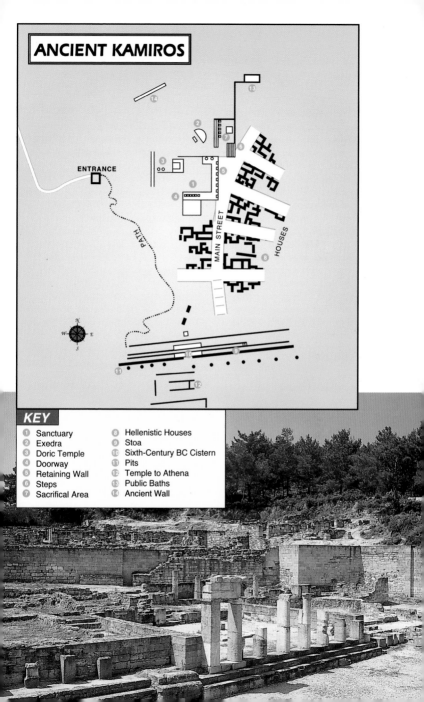

# ANCIENT KAMIROS

**ENTRANCE**

PATH

MAIN STREET

HOUSES

## KEY

1. Sanctuary
2. Exedra
3. Doric Temple
4. Doorway
5. Retaining Wall
6. Steps
7. Sacrifical Area
8. Hellenistic Houses
9. Stoa
10. Sixth-Century BC Cistern
11. Pits
12. Temple to Athena
13. Public Baths
14. Ancient Wall

**Theologos** (Tholos), off the road to the left, has a surprising amount of tourist rooms. There are remains of a temple to Apollo here but it is one for the intrepid history buffs since the excavations are troubled by invading vegetation.

Traffic density increases when **Paradision** and the airport is reached. Although Paradision is virtually on the runway, it does have rooms and tavernas which makes it useful for visitors arriving late or departing very early. It is handy too if there is time to kill at the airport, it is easy to slip over the road to find refreshments or a full meal at Anixis, a family run taverna which offers traditional Greek food and has a good reputation. From here the building density alongside the road increases steadily, particularly noticeable from Kremasti onwards. **Kremasti** is one of the larger villages on the island which has remained Greek and managed to integrate tourism without being overtly touristic. It has hotels and rooms and offers a pebbly beach with the attendant sun parasols and beds. Life stirs on 14 and 15 August with a *panayiria*, a festival for the Assumption of the Virgin Mary with street fairs and a market. In contrast, **Trianda** a little nearer to Rhodes Town has a much heavier and more obvious involvement in tourism and, with over 7,000 inhabitants, is the most populous village on the island outside Rhodes Town. It is also known as Ialysos after the ancient city and both names are in common use. The remains of the ancient city itself up on the hill inland are now known by the modern name of Filerimos.

Heading towards Rhodes Town it is more convenient to look at the coastal area of Trianda first before heading up to Filerimos. A one way system operates which allows a left at the second set of lights which then leads down past tourist shops and tavernas to the sea front. If a good beach is a high priority then the narrow stretch of sand and shingle will disappoint but, nevertheless, it is well decked with sun umbrellas angled against the constant breeze which is meat to the windsurfers. Looking northwards, there are views down the coast to Rhodes Town. Hotels are located in areas both on the seaward side and the inland side of the main through road and the village is well connected to Rhodes by bus.

For Filerimos, follow the one way system back to the main road and continue across at the traffic lights. Open countryside is not far away which is appreciated as the road winds and twists up the pine clad slopes of Mount Filerimos occasionally presenting arresting views. There is plenty of space so parking is no problem.

The summit plateau, 876ft (267m) was the home of the acropolis of the ancient city of Ialysos, one of the three ancient cities of the island. The city itself spread over the north-western slopes towards the village of Kremasti but now interest centres only on the summit plateau.

# Ialysos through the Ages

π

Known as **Filerimos** since the Middle Ages, previously called Ialysos and referred to by the ancients as Archaia, even the name causes confusion but it does hold clues to its origins.

According to legend and to votive offerings found during excavations, this fertile area was first occupied by the Phoenicians from a very early period. Later, around 1500, the Minoans arrived from Crete to set up trading posts and they too chose Ialysos only to be superseded a century later by the Mycenaean Archaeans. It was the style of Mycenaeans to build strong fortresses, usually on a hill, to guard an area of fertile land and the plateau on Mount Filerimos was the ideal place. Many centuries later, long after the Mycenaeans had fallen to the Dorian invaders around the twelfth century BC, the memory was kept alive by the use of the name Archaia for the acropolis of Ialysos.

Remains of Mycenaean settlements have been found around Trianda and a large number of tombs from the same period have been discovered on the surrounding low hills.

The Dorians, who spoke a form of Greek, were invaders from the north who swept down into Greece and spread to the islands. A regression followed their arrival in which material wealth declined, the art of writing was lost, no building of significance took place and the population shrank. When Greece grew out of this dark age and progressed again, Ialysos, like Kamiros and Lindos, started to flourish and did so until 408BC when the three cities agreed to combine and build a new city, Rhodes. Its history did not finish there. A large temple to Athena Polias and Zeus Polieus was built on the acropolis around the third or second century BC and this, it is believed was built on the site of an earlier temple. Even earlier was the Doric fountain, uncovered by a landslip in 1926, built around the fourth century BC.

An early fifth or sixth century AD Christian basilica obliterated part of the old temple and hastened its destruction. Later the ancient acropolis was used for military purposes first by the Byzantines when they were besieged by the Genoans in 1248 and then by the Knights. It was their first stronghold when they arrived on the island in 1306. The Knights improved the fortifications and built a monastery and a church on the site of the old basilica. The present day monastery with its courtyard and cells was restored by the Italians.

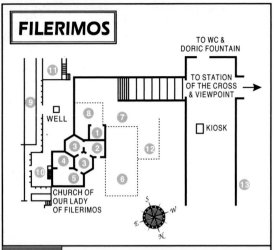

# FILERIMOS

TO WC &
DORIC FOUNTAIN

TO STATION
OF THE CROSS
& VIEWPOINT

KIOSK

WELL

CHURCH OF
OUR LADY
OF FILERIMOS

S
W
E
N

## KEY

1. Early Christian Church
2. d'Aubusson Chapel
3. Two Small Chapels
4. Large Chapel
5. Early Christian Fish Mosaic
6. Temple of Athena and Zeus Polieus
7. Slates: Probably Phoenician
8. Baptistry, Early Christian Church
9. Cloisters
10. Stairway To Pulpit
11. Refectory
12. Subterranean Chapel
13. Ruins of Byzantine Church

*opposite; The rebuilt
Church of Our Lady
of Filerimos*

*The delightful
harbour at
Kamiros Skala*

From the entrance, a stepped avenue shaded by cypress leads up to the rebuilt Church of Our Lady of Filerimos and the monastery. The church has four chapels, the outer of which was built by Grand Master **d'Aubusson** (2) and the innermost still has the floor of the original early Christian church with the **mosaic fish decoration** (5). Solitude reigns in the **cloister** (9) at the rear of the church where the monks cells are each marked with a plaque, each showing a different flower. The remains in front of the church are those of the **Temple of Athena Polias and Zeus Polieus** (6). This temple was a larger version of the one at Lindos with a vestibule entrance guarded by four columns and an enclosed section at the rear, also with four columns. The remains of a paved floor of an even older Phoenician temple can be seen in front of one of the rectangular statue bases.

In front of the temple to Athena is the small underground **Byzantine chapel of Agios Georgios** (12) whose walls were decorated with frescos by the Knights of St John around the fourteenth to fifteenth century.

Returning to the head of the stepped avenue, turning left here leads down to the remains of the Doric fountain which was luckily revealed after a landslip in 1926. It was a highly ornamental roofed fountain built around the fourth century BC with a façade of Doric columns. The water reached the fountain by a channel cut in the rock behind and was delivered through two of the four lion's heads, the other two were ornamental. There were more lion's heads at the front of the basin. A now illegible inscription on one of the posts laid down the law about the use of the fountain.

Back at the head of the stepped avenue, the way opposite the church is a road called Calvary (Golgotha) lined by fourteen copper reliefs representing the Stations of the Cross erected by the Italians. It leads to a platform viewpoint looking over the western side of the island. Absorbing views include the two airports, Trianda, Kremasti, and Maritsa whilst looking to the distance, the two highest points on the island, the wooded slopes of Profitis Ilias and the barren summit of Ataviros, can both be picked out. Available at the on-site shop is a speciality of Filerimos, the seven herb liqueur.

Heading northwards again towards Rhodes Town, **Trianda** merges seamlessly with **Ixia**, the appearance of giant hotels announcing the change. Here are most of the luxury class hotels on the island, the huge Rodos Palace Hotel with bungalows scattered throughout its grounds, the Olympic Palace, a huge crescent shaped hotel with 1,200 rooms, the Hotel Cosmopolitan, the list seems endless but with a busy main road outside the door and a poor, often crowded, beach beyond, all attempt to make their hotel into a complete resort. At night the scene is very different, with bright lights along the road and tavernas, shops and restaurants vying to attract custom from the strolling crowds.

Rhodes Town lies straight ahead but motorists crossing over to the east coast and wishing to avoid Rhodes town can turn right at the traffic lights outside the Rodos Palace Hotel. At the top of the hill turn right and keep ahead, ignoring the complicated traffic system on the left, apart from watching for joining traffic. Keep ahead until past the large Eurospar supermarket on the right then fork off left along the road signposted Asgourou. At the T junction turn left and immediately right to continue ahead. Just at the T junction on the right is another excellent Greek restaurant, To Steki. The next junction is Lindos Avenue main road where a left turn leads back to Rhodes Town and a right heads south towards Faliraki and Lindos. Using this route in reverse is equally convenient but the complicated traffic system can cause confusion on first acquaintance with its cluster of no entry signs. It is nothing more than a disguised roundabout where a left with the traffic flow followed by a right and an immediate left leads down to the Rodos Palace Hotel and the coast road.

# Additional Information

## Places to Visit

### Monolithos
*Castle*
Open site, no admission charge.

### Kritinia
*Castle*
Open site, no admission charge.

### Ancient Site Kamiros
Open: daily 8.30am-3pm, closed Monday. There is an admission charge every day except on Sunday when it is free.

### Filerimos
Ialysos
Open: daily 8.30am-3pm, closed Monday. There is an admission charge every day except on Sunday when it is free.

## Accommodation

### IXIA: TELEPHONE PREFIX 0241

*Grecotel Rodos Imperial* (L)
☎ 75000

*Miramare Beach Hotel* (L)
☎ 24251-4

*Olympic Palace* (L)
☎ 28755

*Rodos Palace Hotel & Bungalows* (De Luxe)
☎ 25222

*Hotel Avria Beach* (A)
☎ 25284

*Belair Beach Hotel* (A)
☎ 23731-4

*Blue Bay Hotel & Apartments* (A)
☎ 92352

*Hotel Cosmopolitan* (A)
☎ 35373

*Electra Palace* (A)
☎ 92521

*Hotel Elina* (A)
☎ 92944

*Hotel Golden Beach* (A)
☎ 92411

*Soaking up the sun around the pool at Rodos Palace Hotel, Ixia*

*Metropolitan Capsis Hotel &*
*Apartments* (A)
☎ 25015

*Rodos Bay Hotel* (A)
☎ 23662

*Apollonia Apartments* (A)
☎ 92951

*Elisabeth Apartments* (A)
☎ 92656

*Maribel Apartments* (A)
☎ 93348

*Possidonia Apartments* (A)
☎ 22276

*Hotel Leto* (B)
☎ 23511

*Hotel Solemar* (B)
☎ 22941

*Alia Apartments* (B)
☎ 31410

*Wing Apartments* (B)
☎ 32361

*Hotel Roma* (C)
☎ 24447

*Hotel Vellois* (C)
☎ 24615

*Blue Eyes Apartments* (C)
☎ 36797

*Pefka Pension* (C)
☎ 93388

**KREMASTI: TELEPHONE**
**PREFIX 0241**

*Filerimos, Hotel & Bungalows* (A)
☎ 92933

*Filerimos Apartments* (A)
☎ 92510

*Armonia Apartments* (A)
☎ 93077

*Kremasti Village Apartments* (A)
☎ 92424

*Paleos Apartments* (A)
☎ 92431

*Hotel Sunflower* (B)
☎ 93893

*Hotel Anseli* (C)
☎ 92013

*Esmeralda Apartments* (C)
☎ 94447

*Gennesis Apartments* (C)
☎ 92798

*Margarita Apartments* (C)
☎ 94254

*Valentino Apartments* (C)
☎ 91487

## PARADISION: TELEPHONE PREFIX 0241

*Vallion Village* (B)
☎ 92309

*Maravelias Apartments* (C)
☎ 94210

*Villa Helena Apartments* (C)
☎ 36827

## SORONI: TELEPHONE PREFIX 0241
*Hotel Silia Soronis* (C)
☎ 41025

## THEOLOGOS: TELEPHONE PREFIX 0246

*Hotel Happy Days* (B)
☎ 41632

*Hotel Nirvana Beach* (B)
☎ 41127

*Hotel Sabina* (B)
☎ 41160

*Hotel Alex Beach* (C)
☎ 41159

*Hotel Christina* (C)
☎ 41560

*Hotel Ivory* (C)
☎ 41679

*Hotel Meliton* (C)
☎ 41666

*Hotel Sunset* (C)
☎ 41201

## TRIANDA (IALYSOS): TELEPHONE PREFIX 0241

*Blue Bay Hotel* (A)
☎ 92352

*Hotel Blue Horizon* (A)
☎ 93484

*Electra Palace* (A)
☎ 92521

*Hotel Golden Beach* (A)
☎ 92411

*Ialysos Bay Hotel* (A)
☎ 91841

*Latin Beach Hotel* (A)
☎ 94053

*Hotel Sun Beach* (A)
☎ 93821

*Anita Apartments* (A)
☎ 94258

*Benelux Apartments* (A)
☎ 93716

*Blue Bay Apartments* (B)
☎ 91113

*Cosmos Apartments* (B)
☎ 94080

*Kassandra Apartments* (B)
☎ 94236

*Hotel Matoula Beach* (B)
☎ 94251

*Pachos Apartments* (B)
☎ 92514

*Swan Apartments* (B)
☎ 94502

*Hotel Eleni* (C)
☎ 93717

*Hotel Green View* (C)
☎ 91009

*Hotel Michele* (C)
☎ 30940

*Hotel Tasimara* (C)
☎ 92380

*Hotel Trianda* (C)
☎ 94525

*Arleniko Apartments* (C)
☎ 94255

*Debby Apartments* (C)
☎ 94651

*El Dorado Apartments* (C)
☎ 94021

*Sunday Apartments* (C)
☎ 91921

## *Local Transport*

Siana and Kritinia are not conveniently served by buses to Rhodes town, except for those staying in these villages. A bus leaves Siana early morning to Rhodes Town which calls in at Kritinia and returns in the afternoon.

Skala Kamiros, which it within walking distance of Kritinia, has an early morning bus from Rhodes Town to connect up with the Halki ferry and a return bus in the afternoon.

Ancient Kamiros has its own bus service in season which reaches around five buses per day at the peak.

The route between Rhodes town and the airport has the most frequent service on the island with buses running around half hourly from early morning until late evening. Paradision, Kremasti, Trianda and Ixia all lie on this route.

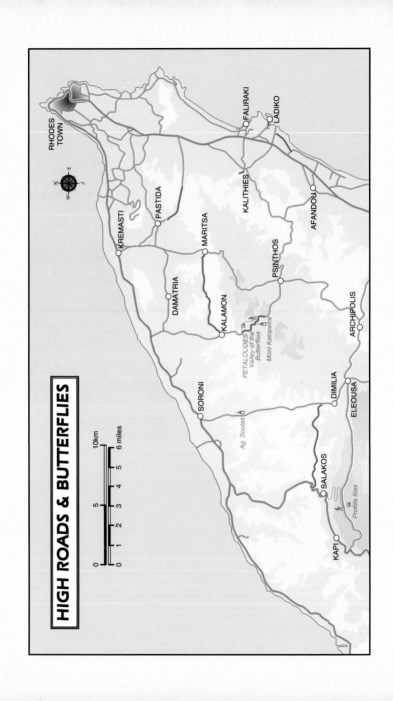

# High Roads &
## Butterflies

**6**

This tour of 77½ miles (125km) explores the local colour and beauty spots in the northern sector of the island. Many of the country villages which lie inland of the coastal road are included as well as the much vaunted Valley of the Butterflies after which it is a gain of altitude for the heights of Profitis Ilias, the second highest mountain on the island.

One or two of the villages close to Rhodes Town, like Maritsa and Pastida, have somehow escaped inclusion to the regular tourist trail and certainly do not feature on the ubiquitous 'round the island' tour so popular with tour operators and visitors alike. Inevitably some villagers are employed in tourism bringing wealth into the village, but a visit still provides an insight into life and customs of village folk. It is here where the openness, the inquisitiveness and the friendliness of the ordinary Greek people emerges if time is taken to sit and relax amongst them.

Rhodian countryside is at its brightest and most colourful in spring but the softly pine clad hills around Profitis Ilias remain refreshingly green throughout, defying the scorching heat of summer which turns lowlands into an arid desert of dried vegetation. The mountain roads are mostly well surfaced, as are the roads throughout this tour except in a few parts, noticeably between Psinthos and the Valley of the Butterflies.

Leave Rhodes Town by the Lindos road and, once past the Koskinou junction, look for the turn off on the right to Kalithies for the first port of call. Situated in a hollow just out of sight of the sea, **Kalithies** wraps itself around a cross roads where much of the village life takes place. The bars, *kafeneons* and old shops add atmosphere but do not expect to find good Greek food, at least not in summer. The only taverna, O Kantas, closes for the summer and reopens in Faliraki near Hotel Colombia but there is fast food to be found. Western style fast food is catching on somewhat alarmingly with the Greek youth and fast foods places, like Fat Boy here, are turning up where least expected. Kalithies is the dormitory for Faliraki workers and its population includes a fair number of expatriates who started as summer workers but have now settled in the village.

For the onward route to Psinthos, turn sharp left at the cross roads in the centre of the village and shortly right following the signs. From here it is a run through quiet countryside where the road winds and twists through small interior valleys turning again when confronted by another hillock. Ignore the road off left to Afandou after 3 miles (5km) and keep meandering towards **Psinthos**, reached after a further 4 miles (6km). A huge central square overlooked by the church and several tavernas dominates the village. There is no air of prosperity here but new buildings on the outskirts may soon change that. Recently, it has become a favoured village for organised Greek evenings, especially in early season before Embonas warms up enough in the evening to provide competition. The road to Valley of the Butterflies, the next port of call, is signposted off to the right just before the village square is reached. Climbing gradually into pine woods on a good surface, all might seem plain sailing but some care is needed where the hard surface ends and the road continues as stabilised track. Moni Kalopetra, startlingly white in the glare of the sun, is reached just before the descent to the Valley of the Butterflies. The monastery has a peaceful courtyard with picnic tables where the countryside can be overlooked in quiet contemplation, perhaps with a drink since light refreshments are available.

Descent through the woodlands leads very shortly to the car park for Petaloudes, the Valley of the Butterflies. Densely wooded and penetrated by a trickling stream, this valley is the summer resting place of an attractive butterfly (or rather moth, see feature box on page 131) and they normally arrive by their thousands. It is a beauty spot in its own right and has been managed as such with walkways, water-

*preceding page; Dimilia church*

## Petaloudes to Moni Kalopetra on Foot

This short walk explores the **Valley of the Butterflies** and continues beyond to wind up to the monastery where refreshments can be taken before heading back the same way. Much of the walk is on fairly good footpaths but sensible shoes or trainers are strongly recommended. Allow around 1 hour for the complete walk.

From the pay box at the Valley of the Butterflies set off uphill following the footpaths through this densely shaded valley. Keep on the main footpath by the stream, constantly ascending through the valley. Leave the Valley of the Butterflies through the unguarded green gate at the top and follow the footpath to meet a woodland track around 3 minutes later. Turn right onto this track and keep going until prevented by a large gate but pass through the personal gate and continue on the track to pass below the monastery before meeting a major track where a left turn leads directly to the monastery. Return the same way.

falls, rock pools, rustic bridges and resting places. Petaloudes is open for virtually the whole of the tourist season even though the butterflies are only actually present from late June until the end of August.

From the car park the valley runs both uphill and down with the major section uphill from the pay box. There is a restaurant/café complex at the lowest level.

From here fast roads are used to proceed towards the mountain area of Profitis Ilias. Head downhill, passing through Kalamon, to reach the west coast and turn left. Follow the coast road through Soroni and be prepared to turn left towards Apollona once through the town. Drive this narrow road through light cultivation keeping an eye open for the left turn just 2 miles (4km) along for **Ag Soulas**. Although the chapel might be tiny, the grounds are extensive with a taverna, a play area and a race track! The taverna opens infrequently, usually high days, holidays and any time a crowd gathers. Crowds do gather, especially on the 29 and 30 July, the chapel's saints day, for a large festival which includes a major attraction unique on the island, donkey racing!

Continuing towards Dimilia, watch out for the stabilised track on the right leading to Salakos, it is reached just 3 miles (5km) after rejoining the road from the monastery. Apart from being a little dusty, it is a good track to drive which soon reveals views of the cypress and pine wooded Profitis Ilias and of the Italianate buildings near the summit soon to be visited. It takes a careful scrutiny to pick out the zig-zag path ascending the side of the mountain from Salakos towards the

The short walk between Petaloudes (above) and
Moni Kalopetra (below) explores the Valley of the Butterflies

# Butterflies of the Valley

There is no argument that the butterflies are really moths but this tiny deception pays handsomely since a Valley of the Moths title lacks that air of romanticism to draw the crowds. Fortunately, the red and black Jersey tiger moth, *Euplagia quadripunctaria*, is attractive and has the distinction of being the only moth in the world to become a major tourist attraction. Thousands arrive in the height of summer, July and August, settling on the tree trunks and on the mossy rocks for a period of aestivation but this resting is frequently disturbed by the coach loads of visitors clapping their hands to watch the cloud of moths rise from the trees. This continual disturbance has led to a reduction in the numbers returning to the valley in recent years and noisy activities, like clapping and the blowing of whistles are now banned.

Why the moths come to this particular valley has never been clearly understood. Certainly the valley offers the moths a cool moist haven but the particular trees present, *Liquidambar orientalis*, which also thrives in the damp conditions, are believed to be important. These trees, exude drops of 'liquid amber' sweet gum from the bark which may attract them.

The trees are often wrongly referred to as styrax or storax but this may arise from a confusion with the closely related *Liquidambar styraciflua*, a North American native, which is called styrax or storax. To add to the confusion *Styrax officinalis*, a white flowered shrub also called styrax or storax, does grow on Rhodes but not necessarily in this valley.

*Wild flowers such as* Cyclamen repandum *can be found on Rhodes*

summit buildings. This is an old *kalderimi* (cobbled path) which was once the main route for taking provisions to the top by donkey and is now a popular route for walkers. See the feature box on page 133 for details.

When the track meets the road turn left for Salakos which is soon reached.

Salakos has a small platia alongside the main road. Shaded by trees, it is a great place to twiddle the worry beads and sit in contemplation of the world and its people. The onward route out west is graced by the wooded slopes of the mountain rising away to the left where cypress slowly gives way to pine. Turn left after 3 miles (5km) and continue climbing to drive on the highest road on the island through green and flower decked fields towards the summit of Profitis Ilias. Park when the chalet buildings are reached.

**Profitis Ilias**, after the Prophet Elijah, is not just the name of the monastery but of the mountain and the settlement on top. The two adjacent Swiss Chalet style hotels, Elafos (stag) and Elafina (doe), were built by the Italians. Now looking distinctly jaded, they have actually been closed for a number of years but, in spite of this, they still manage to find their way into hotel lists for the island. In front of the hotels is, appropriately, a deer enclosure. The walled-in monastery itself is small and shows little signs of life until 20 June, its Saint's day.

Uphill of the road, the large chalet building which was built for the Italian Governor now stands deserted with its doors and windows flapping in the breeze. To the right is a small chapel, from where it is possible to follow the footpaths laid out by the Italians in a circular walk up and along the summit ridge, for sparkling views over Apollona, and down again at the eastern end. The summit itself, occupied by the army, is not accessible. Steps from the road side lead into the small café which serves the finest yoghurt and honey on the island and there is no more relaxing place to enjoy it than on the wooden terrace outside.

At this altitude, the wild flowers can be enjoyed a little later into the season than at lower levels and it is possible to see *Cyclamen repandum*, which is widespread up here, until late May and possibly later in a cool spring. One speciality to look out for which is fairly common here but not in other parts of the island, is the charming, white *Paeonia clusii ssp rhodia*. It flowers in April and May and can sometimes be seen on the banks overhanging the road.

The onwards drive to Eleousa through the cool, green forests passes the fourteenth-century Byzantine church of Agios Nikolaos Foundoukli (St Nicholas of the Hazelnuts) with its interesting wall paintings. It is believed that the hillsides here were once covered with hazelnuts.

Entering **Eleousa**, a road system guides traffic through the old Italianate Plaza, now a crumbling edifice. Built originally as a palace

# Salakos to Profitis Ilias by Kalderimi

This most direct route from Salakos to the top of Profitis Ilias follows an old *kalderimi* (cobbled trail), which wends its way up the mountain side. Even though there is a fair ascent involved, the generous sweeps of the zig-zag ensure that no section is particularly steep and the walking is fairly easy.

Starting from the platia in the centre of Salakos, follow the main road out west towards Embonas until past the restaurant/hotel on the left reached after just a few minutes. From here look for a narrow concrete road on the left just where the main road bends sharply right and just before the orange bus shelter. Follow the narrow road/track for just over a minute to locate a rough track leading off to the left, indicated by a spot of red paint on a rock. This track heads in the direction of the mountain and soon connects to the old trail but there are two forks to negotiate first: ignore the first and keep up but bear left at the second following the more obvious route. By now the trail is firmly established and all that is necessary is to follow through the cypress and pine trees that cloak the landscape catching views down to Salakos from time to time.

Amongst the scent of pine, spring walkers can enjoy a feast of wild flowers like the dainty white cyclamen, *C. repandum* which can be found in bloom from March at the lower levels through until late May at the top or a feast of wild orchids like the elegant, slender *Orchis anatolica* or the strikingly marked bee orchid, *Ophrys reinholdii*. Also found along here, and rather surprisingly since it tends to favour coastal locations, is the mandrake, *Mandragora officinalis*, often called the mystic mandrake. Its large wrinkled leaves form a rosette which lies close to the ground and its small pale blue flowers are followed by orange berries. It is a plant full of folk lore to which many properties have been assigned through the ages, including its use as an aphrodisiac which is mentioned in the Bible. There is a little more of the folklore which perhaps should not be ignored; the shriek emitted when the forked roots are pulled from the ground is a harbinger of death to those within earshot!

The chapel of St Anthony lies above but there is no clear view of it until the trail levels out at the top of the hill and starts to head away from the face. Keep the chapel on the right and once beyond keep right to join a woodland track. To visit the chapel and enjoy the solitude and views from its terrace turn right, otherwise turn left and follow the woodland track until the monastery of Profitis Ilias comes into view. Head for this and from here the main buildings on the top are all accessible. Return down to Salakos by the same route.

# The Pine Processionary Caterpillar

The nests seen dripping from pine trees both here and along many of the Mediterranean coasts and islands in Greece are full of the Pine Processionary Caterpillar, *Thaumetopoea pityocampa*. They live in these communal nests through the winter and come out to feed only when the weather is warm enough. Their communal behaviour persists even on leaving the nest and they move in procession, each one in contact nose to tail with the next to form

chains extending to several metres in length. When fully grown, which is usually by late spring or early summer, they pupate in cocoons below ground and emerge as moths later in the summer. Eggs are laid in large numbers around the pine needles and are covered by scales from the body of the female. The reproductive cycle is completed in the course of one year.

A word of warning; these dark brown caterpillars are covered in hairs which are highly irritant and will cause a painful rash if they come into contact with the skin.

*In Maritsa school children await English lessons. It was also a name day so the children are carrying gifts for the teacher*

for the governor, it later became a barracks for Greek troops and part of it still is used by the military. Situated on the slopes of the summit region, Eleousa offers a shady platia with a number of tavernas and snack bars which sometimes attracts tour coaches to disgorge there.

**Archipolis** is the next port of call and the road there is still flanked by pines. A filling station is the first building encountered; it is one of the few around in these mountain villages. Archipolis was designed to serve the traveller. It sits astride the road offering cafés and tavernas to the wayfarer. The ochre church with its wedding cake style campanile fights for its own space amongst the houses.

On leaving Archipolis, watch out for the left turn to Psinthos in 2 miles (4km) which is indicated but with a somewhat battered sign easy to miss. The road is narrow and surfaced but full of potholes for much of the way to Psinthos, probably about the worst surfaced road on the island. One redeeming feature is that it is a scenic run through descending foothills, occasionally crossing narrow bridges. A road side taverna reached before Psinthos marks an improvement of the road surface. Continue through Psinthos on the road to Maritsa. The route winds back up into the mountains which shelters Petaloudes and the scenery is reminiscent of it in parts. Although short, this is one of the most scenic runs on the island as the road flirts in high drama around mountain tops revealing glimpses down to lower regions from time to time.

**Maritsa** is one of those places tempting only to drive straight through since it seems to have no identifiable centre. It must be explored on foot. The back streets provide some of those images which are characteristically Greek, old ladies in black sitting on doorsteps, flower pots on whitewashed steps, green shuttered windows, flower decked balconies and outside ovens. The *kafeneon* too has an old atmosphere and serves up some typically Greek *mezedes* with drinks, wine or ouzo.

The tour concludes with a visit to **Pastida** before returning to Rhodes Town. Pastida is now another of those dormitory villages supported by tourism without being directly engaged in it. One claim to fame is the bread shop on the road out to Kalithies. Locals insist that it bakes the best bread on the island.

For Rhodes Town leave Pastida and head towards Kremasti and the coast road. For east coast destinations, take the Kalithies road which shortly runs into a new wide road which is intended eventually to carry traffic from the airport to the east coast. The first part of the road is unsurfaced but the surfaced section is soon reached. It meets up with the main Lindos avenue mid-way between the Koskinou junction to the north and the Kalithies junction to the south.

# Additional Information

## Places to Visit

**Petaloudes**
*Valley of the Butterflies*
Open: 8am-7pm. Entrance charge.

## Accommodation

**SALAKOS: TELEPHONE PREFIX 0246**
*Nimfi Pension* (B)
☎ 22206
There are no major hotels in any of the villages visited. Some may have rooms and the best place to enquire is in the village taverna or *kafeneon*.

## Transport

The villages close to Rhodes Town, Maritsa, Pastida, Kalathies all have a regular daily bus service. For outlying villages, the situation is far less good. Psinthos has two buses, one morning the other afternoon and Archipolis also has two, both morning departures, 6am and 7.30am for Rhodes Town and returning from Rhodes at 1.15pm and 3.15pm.

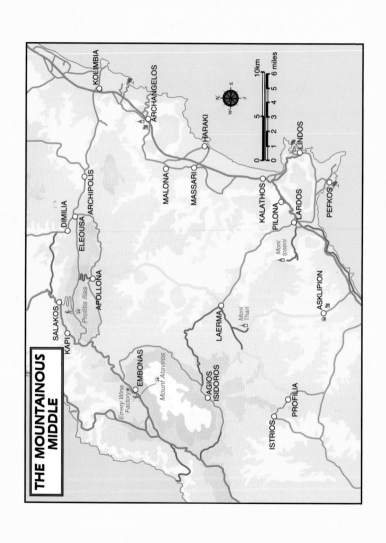

# THE MOUNTAINOUS MIDDLE

# The Mountainous Middle

# 7

A circuit around the skirts of Mount Ataviros, the highest mountain range on the island, a visit to Embonas, the highest village, a chance to taste wines and a couple of monasteries are amongst the highlights on this 112 mile (180km) tour. Although well surfaced roads are used in the main, there are two stretches, from the west coast road towards Agios Isidoros and again from Agios Isidoros to Laerma which are only stabilised track and are slower to drive. The latter track is not recommended after heavy rain.

The central part of the island exists on an uneasy alliance between forestry, small scale farming and animal husbandry. Much of the region is covered by forest or scrubland with only a few areas suitable for farming. From the commercial point of view, the forests are not luxurious enough for exploitation and they provide relatively small amounts of low grade timber suitable only for fuel. Often sheep and goats are the mainstay of life in these country areas and provide milk for yoghurt and cheese as well as meat. Goats will survive in areas of meagre vegetation where other livestock would fail but overgrazing by these animals is in itself destructive in not allowing regeneration so creating a vicious circle which is difficult to break and condemns the farmer to a poor living. If there is prosperity in the region then it is at **Embonas**. Here altitude, climatic and soil factors combine to make it the best region on the island for growing vines and here too is the location of Emery, one of two major wine manufacturers on the island. Success builds upon success, Embonas' colourful village life and high location makes a focal point for tourism, particularly for the round the island tours and organised Greek evenings. The sense of isolation of this central section is most keenly observed on part of the return leg from Agios Isidoros to Lardos via Laerma.

Leave Rhodes town on the Lindos road and continue heading south past Faliraki and the Ladiko junction. The absorbing view down the coast immediately past here, of the long sweep of the bay terminating in four distinct mountains layered one on another, vies with the view of the offshore islands on the west coast as the finest on the island. The innermost mountain here marks the Kolimbia junction on the route of this tour where a right turn towards Archipolis is required. Looking across the wide river bed immediately on turning gives a momentary view of the disused old bridge which was formerly the route of the main road. The river bed is followed up the valley for a time until past the Epta Pigis turn off. If this was not visited in Chapter 2, there is another opportunity now. Woodlands start to enclose the road as it winds in gentle ascent and leads almost unexpectedly into a clearing in front of the monastery of Ag Nectarios. An archway leads to steps up to the grandiose Byzantine style church guarded by columnar cypress trees. The separate campanile, with a tiered construction, is borrowed from a later period. Picnic tables are provided just outside the church. See also the feature box on page 141.

Pine forest still dominates the onward journey which leads through Archipolis (visited in Chapter 6) and on to Eleousa. Turn left here towards Apollona keeping south of the main Profitis Ilias summit region while heading towards the distant, barren massive of Ataviros. A dip in the road, a bend and tiny **Platania** is passed before there is time for a glance. The eye-catching Byzantinesque white church of St Peter and Paul on the right distracts from the Laerma junction on the left. Laerma is visited on this tour but by a different route so it is straight on to Apollona for now. **Apollona** is altogether a more substantial village and one worth a stop to look around. Outside ovens are still used here and visitors fortunate enough to be passing through before Easter time might find themselves with a handful of the freshly baked Easter biscuits. The ovens are still used for cooking as well as for making bread and the Panorama Restaurant is the place to sample some oven cooked food. There is a small folk museum too if you can catch it open.

*preceding page; The Byzantine white church of St Peter and Paul at Laerma junction with Mount Ataviros in the distance*

## Churches and Monasteries

Throughout a long and turbulent history, the church on Rhodes has been at the heart of society and provided an enduring constancy which bonds people even today. The buildings, many from the thirteenth and fourteenth century or earlier, offer a strand of historical and social comment but equally fascinating is the difference in architectural styles which have developed in its isolation from Greece, styles which are not seen elsewhere outside the Dodecanese.

The most obvious of these is the tiered campanile standing separately from the main church building and sometimes used as the entrance gate. Simpler examples, like Moni Skiadi, have just two tiers under a small roof dome, but those on a grander scale, and one of the best examples is at Archangelos, may have six or seven ever decreasing tiers. Almost invariably white, they offer one of the lasting impressions of the island. Another fairly distinctive feature is the cross-vaulting in the roof and few of the modern churches are without it.

Religious pilgrimage is a major form of tourism amongst the Greek people who are prepared to travel island to island to see famous ikons or monasteries. Many of the monasteries now recognise this and are responding by building overnight accommodation within the grounds, as at Moni Thari. Even the most humble of the churches and monasteries recognise their social role and encourage their grounds to be used to celebrate festivals and name days and facilities for this are never neglected when expansion plans are in the air.

Myth, folklore and religion are intertwined on Rhodes more than anywhere in Greece and many of the saints are quite local and completely without pedigree. In much the same way, many local customs and superstitions are built in to religious ritual and some of these, like the belief in the evil eye, are a legacy left behind by the Turks.

Grey, imposing **Mount Ataviros**, with a fierce presence but without  character, dominates the skyline with onward progress towards Embonas. It is a mountain which does not invite walkers, it challenges them and many take up the challenge tackling it from the north-west side, just beyond Embonas of which more shortly. Turn left at the junction reached 5 miles (8km) on from Apollona for the final run into **Embonas**. The first major building on the right, on entering the village is the **Emery** wine factory which is happy to receive visitors between  9am and 3.20pm on weekdays. Drive in through the main gate and park in the big yard, enter the factory through the personal door and walk the length of the shed past all the stainless steel vessels and turn right at the end into the bar reception area. Here casual visitors can enjoy a complimentary wine tasting session at the bar whereas groups have special tables set aside for them. The quieter times for casual visitors are before 10am and after 2pm between these hours is a succession of coach parties.

## Emery Wines

Located at the heart of the vine region on the island, Emery is on hand to work closely with the farmers in advising and selecting vineyards which produce the most suitable grapes. The region around Embonas is cooled by altitude and by winds funnelled from the west which produce very local microclimates. Throw the soil factor into the equation and the result is that particular vineyards in the region are superior to others in the quality of grape produced. Two grape varieties are prominent here, the Athiri grape for the white wine and the Amorgianos for the red.

Harvest time lasts around 3 weeks, from late August into September and the subsequent fermentation stage also lasts about 2 to 3 weeks. The white wine is ready in one year but the better quality red wine (Cava) is stored in oak casks for 6 months then bottled and stored for up to 3 years. Italian wine tasters are used to help maintain quality.

Their wine list includes:
*Emery dry white:* served chilled, this is an excellent dry, slightly fruity wine which, at its price, is the best of the island's white wines.
*Emery demi-sec white:* only slightly sweeter than the dry with much of the character.
*Emery Rose:* another excellent wine.
*Castel de Rhodes:* lacks subtlety, red wine drinkers might be disappointed.
*Emery Cava red:* top of range and matured in oak, not usually available for testing. Similarly two other labels, Villare dry white and Granrose Emery.
Yamas! (cheers!)

Embonas village has a disproportionate number of tavernas for its size. It is famed on the island for the quality of its meat which makes it a natural target for a lunch stop, either before or after wine tasting, on every single round-the-island tour offered. Many coaches are back again in the evening for the organised Greek evening so popular with holidaymakers. The village has blossomed both tavernas and tourist shops to satisfy the passing trade. For the casual visitor, it is extremely difficult to find a quiet spot for lunch for a couple of hours following mid-day. One place to try is the Hasapotaverna, the butcher's taverna. To find it head up the taverna lined street towards the church and the Two Brothers' Hasapotaverna lies just past with part outside the butchers shop and more over the road. There is another local wine producer in Embonas who markets a red wine full of character called Alexandros and this may be an opportunity to try it. The village has managed to retain some of its character and the local costume is sometimes worn by the older people. Winter is the time for villagers to concentrate on their handicrafts, particularly lace and hand made carpets, which are prominent in the tourist shops throughout summer.

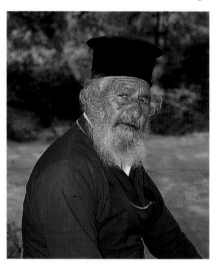

*The village priest is a familiar site in the local community*

Continue the tour by driving through Embonas heading out towards the west coast. Just outside, particularly where a track runs off left, is one of the more spectacular views of the steep face of Mount Ataviros. Looking at the face of the mountain, there are three gulley-like depressions descending from near the summit and the route for walkers climbs up the central one. It takes almost 3 hours to reach the top and a similar time to come down but it is not a walk for the inexperienced. At the top, and which few people get to see, are the remains of a temple dedicated to Zeus. Built of local stone, it blends so well it is almost imperceptible but the most significant part is a side wall built in large rectangular blocks.

There is a new stretch of road ahead which has not yet reached the commercial maps but is indicated on the map here. Where the road forks, on the way to join the coast road, keep left which is effectively ahead on the new road. Both roads actually lead to the coast road and the one to the right is useful for those heading north. Turn left on reaching the coast road and spare a moment to enjoy the view of the offshore islands north to south, and nearest, are the small islands of Makri, Strongili and Tragoussia; still north to south, more distant and larger are Alimnia and Halki. It is one of the finest viewpoints on the island and the vision of those islands floating in a colourwash of blue is almost surreal. There is more than one occasion to enjoy the offshore views on the run south before the turn off right onto the unsurfaced road to Agios Isidoros, after 4 miles (6km). It is a good stabilised track becoming surfaced road, after 2 miles (3km), which winds around the contours and remains good all the way to **Agios Isidoros**. This is a small village built on the steep lower slopes of Mount Ataviros and full of snack bars. It is so steeply tiered in places that a walk down through the village gives mostly views of roof tops and chimneys and, in places, it is easily possible to walk from the street straight onto a flat roof. If the Papas is around, there is little chance of avoiding a visit to the church to see the finely carved pulpit bearing the name of the craftsman. So enthusiastic is the Papas, he seems totally oblivious to dress which other churches would regard as improper!

Once through Agios Isidoros, look for the track right leading to Laerma. Progress slows for the next 7 miles (11km) until **Laerma** is reached. Although in the main the track is good, there are parts which are rough and need to be taken slowly. It is a slow, steady descent through one of the more remote regions of the island. Cradled in the hills in splendid isolation, Laerma, with a population of around 650, is only slightly smaller than Agios Isidoros. Turn right in the centre of the village for a short side trip to one of the ecclesiastical treasures of

## Wild Orchids of Rhodes

The island is blessed with a rich orchid flora which graces the spring months from March, and perhaps earlier for one or two species, through until late May. These are the terrestrial orchids which have their bulbous roots in the ground and not the exotic epiphytics of hotter, steamier climes which are popular for greenhouse cultivation.

In distribution the orchids are just about everywhere where cultivation and grazing pressure allows. Mostly, they have a preference for limestone geology so these regions have a greater number of species. Even so, some areas on the island are richer in orchids than others. One of these is alongside the road to Epta Pigis, close to the Kolimbia junction and another is the summit area around Profitis Ilias. Altitude has a significant influence on flowering times so the sea level site near Kolimbia junction, for example, needs to be explored in March and early April whilst the cooler high altitude site at Profitis Ilias might yield orchid discoveries into late May. For those who thrill at finding wild orchids, the best two weeks when the greatest number of species are in flower at the same time is the first two in April although there is some small seasonal variation.

Orchids have a remarkably consistent botanical structure which irritates the botanist because the usual technique of flower identification, a detailed examination of the reproductive parts followed by the application of a diagnostic key, does not apply. To the absolute delight of the lay man, the best course lies in matching with a picture so with a good book in hand, like *Buttler's Field Guide to Orchids of Britain and Europe*, and with a little experience it is easy to become an expert.

the island, **Moni Thari**. It starts as road but reverts to good stabilised track once outside the village. There is a signposted left fork to reach the monastery which was built around the thirteenth century on much earlier foundations and offers some fine, old frescos. The north and south walls are the oldest, twelfth century, part of the building but some ninth-century remains can be seen in the surrounding grounds. The dome, the apse and the nave all carry frescos of exceptional craftsmanship. Some parts of the wall have as many as four layers of painting, the earliest from 1100. The apse has three layers. Centuries after construction, it is now expanding with the addition of sleeping accommodation. It is a quiet and tempting place to picnic with facilities on hand, unless there is a festival in full swing. The 21 and 22 May is one of those occasions.

And it's back to Laerma which has the distinction of being the village closest to the geographical centre of the island. The onward road to Lardos is at least surfaced although it does get narrow in parts.

---

The islands fifty or so species are dominated by the bee orchids (*genus Ophrys*) and the *genus Orchis*. Bee orchids, with each flower resembling some species of bee or wasp, are usually the most difficult to spot. Often not taller than 23cm (9in), their slender stems carrying perhaps three or four flowers blend in amongst the vegetation with ease. Almost as difficult to spot are the slender spikes of the *Orchis genus* but with a good array of flowers they can be more eye-catching.

Some of the island's orchids which are not difficult to find are listed below:

| | |
|---|---|
| *Genus Ophrys* | *O. anatolica* |
| *O. fusca* | *O. italica* |
| *O. lutea ssp galilaea* | *O. provincialis* |
| *O. tenthredinifera* | *O. lactea* |
| *O. iricolour* | *O. laxiflora* |
| *O. omegaifera* | *O. coriophora* |
| *O. ciliata* | *O. sancta* |
| *O. mammosa* | |
| *O. scolopax* | Others: |
| *O. bornmulleri* | *Aceras anthropophorum* |
| *O. regis-ferdinandii* | *Anacamptis pyramidalis* |
| *O. holoserica* | *Barlia robertiana* |
| *O. holoserica ssp heterochilia* | *Limodorum arbortivum* |
| *O. heldreichii* | *Neotinea maculata* |
| *O. reinholdii* | *Serapias vomeracea* |
| *O. ferrum-equinum* | *Serapias vomeracea* |
| *Genus Orchis:* |   *ssp orientalis* |
| *O. papilionacea* | *Serapias vomeracea* |
| |   *ssp laxiflora* |

Well outside Laerma, the fields on the right are damp and boggy in winter and spring providing the ideal habitat for certain flowers which are found nowhere else on the island. The most prominent and eye-catching of these is a tall growing purple orchid, *Orchis laxiflora* which grows here in abundance. Rhodes is particularly well blessed with wild orchids and more details are given in the feature box on pages 144-145.

The road follows a ridge for a time affording excellent views over a landscape once devastated by forest fires but now showing signs of regeneration. On entering Lardos head right for a side trip to **Moni Ipseni**. Signposts lead the way and there is a little more track driving through woodland but the surface is well stabilised. Stations of the cross are first glimpsed through the trees and shortly afterwards the monastery is reached. It is of recent construction and unusual in that it is a living, working monastery in the control of an order of nuns who greet visitors kindly and happily show them around. Cool elegance awaits with citrus trees surrounding a fountain in the quiet courtyard. Outside is a large area used for festivities and a white chapel overlooks from a nearby hill.

Return to Lardos and rejoin the coastal road for the journey back to Rhodes Town. If time is not pressing, try the existing sections of the National Road which are a little slower to drive but scenically more interesting. The first section starts off left north of Kalathos and leads through Massari and Malona to Archangelos. Almost immediately on rejoining the main coast road, look again for a left turn which has a sign for Savas Pottery and Rhodes.

## *Additional Information*

### *Places to Visit*

**Embonas**
*Emery Wine Factory*
Open: weekdays 9am-3.20pm.

**Moni Thari**
Open: not always open but available for viewing if someone is around.

**Moni Ipseni**
Open: no regular opening hours but the most reliable time is in the morning.

### *Accommodation*

There are no hotels in any of the country villages but there are rooms and apartments available in Embonas and Lardos, ask in the tavernas and souvenir shops. There is less certainty about the smaller villages but, again, enquire at the cafés.

### *Transport*

The region is poorly served by buses. Embonas has one bus daily which departs the village for Rhodes Town at 7am following the west coast road and returns from Rhodes at 1.15pm. Laerma also has a bus leaving at 7am for Rhodes Town following the east coast road. This returns from Rhodes at 3pm.

# Off The Beaten Track
## Southern Villages

# 8

This tour of 150 miles (242km) explores the lesser visited southernmost section of the island. The eastern coast road, generally much quicker than the western route, is used for both access and the return. Allow about 1½ hours for the drive down from Rhodes Town to Gennadion which is effectively the start of the tour. One section of this tour, from just beyond Apolakia southwards along the west coast, is on an unsurfaced road which is generally sound but should be taken steadily. There is a second 5 mile (8km) section of track from Katavia down to Prasonissi at the very tip of the island which is maintained annually but the treatment is confined to planing to smooth out the winter erosion. Many hire cars use this track but it does need to be taken carefully. Although villages feature strongly in this tour, two of the most remarkable beaches on the island are also visited, one at Plimmiri and the other at island's end, Prasonissi, where the sea laps in from both sides.

High mountains are left behind for hills and plains largely given over to cultivation. Farming is the chief industry of all the villages in the region but agriculture on the island has been a struggle throughout the ages. Many factors have contributed to this: the inability to harness the high winter rainfall for summer irrigation, soil erosion, small plots arising from the necessity for equal land division according to inheritance law and the lack of mechanisation. Under the Italian regime, the Italians tried hard to tackle these problems and a large scale model farm was set up outside Katavia, where the buildings are still to be seen, and staff brought from Italy to teach modern farming methods. Metal windmills were introduced to help recover deep water for irrigation, still seen in some parts of the island, and encouragement was given to increase the usage of fertilisers and agricultural equipment. The Italians actually went much further and expropriated some of the better quality land around Malona and brought in Italian farmers to lead by example. Farming techniques are much improved now but many of the old problems still restrict production. Fields of wheat, oats and barley are common sights around Katavia but melons too are becoming an important crop in some areas, chiefly around Apolakia, and, of course the ubiquitous olive (see feature box on page 149).

Tourism is fairly minimal in the southern region but tourists in hire cars are finding their way around in ever increasing numbers. Filling stations are still thin on the ground so it pays to set off with a full tank but otherwise tourist facilities in the way of cafes and tavernas are not in short supply. Suggestions for a lunch stop include the hill villages of Istrios and Arnitha for a peaceful countryside location or Plimmiri and Prasonissi if a view of the sea takes precedence.

Follow the Lindos road out of Rhodes Town but once through Kalathos, turn right towards Lardos and avoid driving around the Lindos headland which can be very slow on the poor roads. On reaching Gennadion turn right following signs to Apolakia and watch out for potholes on the early stretch. Just 4 miles (7km) along, watch for the left turn to visit the small village of **Vation**. The pace of life is slow here and the sleeping policemen on the entry road ensure that visitors slow down too. Cubic white houses scattered to some predetermined configuration contrive to leave room for a shady village square. Here is the place to enjoy a drink at the Platanos café-ouzeri under the gaze of a few elderly residents idly toying with their worry beads. This quiet backwater is another world and bearing testament to this scene of inactivity are the ruins of a windmill on a nearby hill. Also at the heart of the village is a church with a bell-tower gate.

Back on the main road, entertained perhaps by the electric blue flashes of swooping bee-eaters which are particularly common in this area, the next turn to look out for is a right turn up to the villages of Profilia and Istrios. These lie on a loop road which climbs high into the hills passing through both these villages before rejoining this same

*preceding page; The undulating countryside around Mesanagros*

# The Olive

Known from Crete as early as 3,500BC, the olive has been central to the existence of the Mediterranean peoples for millennia. Although grown primarily for cooking oil it is also used as a lubricant, for lighting, soap making and in ointments and liniments for the skin. The fruit itself, the olive, is also eaten.

The tree is evergreen with leathery lance-shaped leaves which are dark green above and silvery beneath. With age the trunks become knarled and twisted adding considerably to the character of the tree. It takes 4 to 8 years for a tree to start bearing fruit but full production is not reached until after 15 to 20 years and it may then continue for centuries with proper care. The tree is erratic in that not every year produces a good crop, unless a suitable regime of irrigation and feeding is rigorously followed, but more often good crops are expected every other year. Whitish flowers borne in loose clusters arrive in late spring which rely on the wind for pollination. The fruit which follows takes 6 to 8 months to reach full maturity for only then does it give the maximum yield of oil. This means that harvesting takes place throughout the winter months, from December through until March, the perfect complement to working in the tourist season. Fruits for eating are collected before maturity and need special treatment with dilute caustic lye and salt to kill the extreme bitterness. There are hundreds of named varieties of olives, both for oil and for eating, which are propagated from hard wood cuttings or from leaf cuttings under mist propagation.

Olive oil is produced in a selection of grades, the very finest oil from the first pressing is known as virgin oil and this is the grade preferred for salad dressing. It is a good buy to take home too and can be found on the supermarket shelves in 5 litre containers. The second grade of oil is the pure, a blend of virgin oil and refined oil, which is the third grade. Refined oil is made from the lampante grade, so called because it is used for lamp fuel, by treatment to remove the acid, the colour and the odour. Lampante is obtained from a second pressing of the residual pulp.

The wood too is of great value. It is very hard, strongly grained and takes a fine polish, ideal for carving, cabinet work and toys. It is good to as a slow burning fuel and for making charcoal for which the Greeks have a great demand.

Botanically, the olive, *Olea europea*, belongs to the Oleaceae family and has some interesting and familiar relatives like ash, privet, jasmine and lilac.

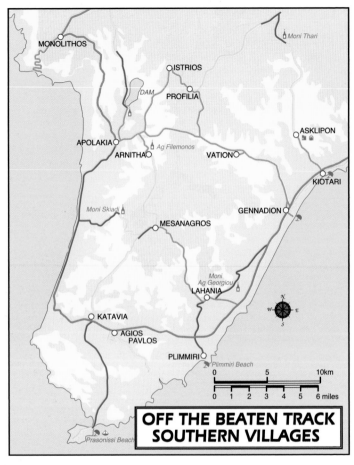

OFF THE BEATEN TRACK
SOUTHERN VILLAGES

main road. It is a steady climb on a good road through forest burnt in earlier fires but now busily regenerating and looking green again. **Profilia**, snuggling in the saddle of a hill and tucked well away from invaders' eyes, is revealed with gaining altitude. White village houses tumble around the hillsides and outside ovens suggest that the way of life is still fairly traditional. From the cool surroundings of the church there are views over to Mount Ataviros. Expansive views on the descent to Istrios encompass the Akramitis range of hills and the village of Siana on its slopes. Cereal crops, golden in the summer sun, have no respect for altitude here. **Istrios**, small and compact, manages a lovely ornamental wooden bus shelter possibly for the benefit of the

*Wayside flowers near Katavia*

*The brightly decorated church at Katavia's*

children awaiting the school bus. El Greco looks an interesting place to eat and boasts Greek specialities as well as an international menu and with a second café-bar restaurant, Valentia, this village is well prepared for visitors. From here it is 4 miles (6km) back to the Apolakia road and, almost immediately after turning right to join it, turn left on a surfaced road for the village of **Arnitha**.

On the left, just before entering the village, is a shady courtyard with a drinking fountain and a taverna which is a quiet place to dine except on a Sunday when the Greeks themselves are out in force. Opposite to this courtyard is the small chapel of Ag Nectarios. Heading into the village still, the monastery of Ag Filemonos with its large courtyard lies up to the left. Before the road bends round to head into the village proper, there is a track off left which connects Arnitha to Mesanagros but is only suitable for four wheel drive vehicles with good clearance. Arnitha itself climbs a steep hillside and is another of those villages best explored on foot to capture all those cameos of flower decked doorways and balconies which are so characteristically Greek.

**Apolakia**, just a short distance away and visited in Chapter 4, gives the impression of a cardboard cut-out image when just passing through with bars and tavernas decorated by immobile figures, rather like a stage set. Turn left at the central junction towards Katavia and make the most of the final stretch of good road before the surface runs out and the road continues as stabilised track. Melon fields are on view around Katavia, one of the major melon growing centres on the island, but civilisation is soon left behind as a wilder stretch of coastline adds a new dimension to the ever changing scenery on this island. Inland, Moni Skiadi, the next port of call, can be seen sitting on a ledge surrounded by fire blackened pine trees. Look for a left turn just 4 miles (6km) out from Katavia, signposted **Moni Skiadi**, and follow this fairly good track into the hills and up to the monastery. The track goes through to Mesanagros but landslides beyond the monastery have made the route impractical for the moment. It matters little for this tour for the intention shortly is to press on down to the southernmost tip of the island.

Moni Skiadi is one of the more important monasteries on the island made famous by its miraculous ikon of the Blessed Virgin (Panagia). Legend tells of a heretic who stabbed the painting many centuries ago and brought blood from the cheek of Mary. Still visible brown stains provide their own persuasive evidence. The ikon is carried around at Easter time from house to house and village to village until it finally comes to rest for a period on the island of Halki. Most of the present buildings arise from the eighteenth and nineteenth centuries built around a thirteenth-century Church of the Holy Cross. In its present form, the tiered campanile is attached to the church building which has a typical cross vaulted roof. Rooms are available for guests wishing to stay overnight but expect it all to be full on 8 September when a *panayiria* is held to celebrate the birth of the Virgin Mary. People from all over the island pilgrimage to the monastery to see the miraculous ikon and to join the celebrations which go on throughout the day and night.

Retrace the route back to the coast road and continue heading south. This section of stabilised road is less comfortable to drive but at least it rejoins surfaced road well before Katavia is reached. At the cross roads where right is signposted Prasonissi, turn left for now into **Katavia**. A short ride leads to the heart of the village, the *platia*, built around a road junction. Café-bars and tavernas cater for the passing tourist trade and, unless temptation is resisted, it is easy to join the Greeks, sit back in the leafy shade and watch the world go by. Those with a little energy left may prefer to wander the back streets to explore the older part of the village. Some of the houses here have imposing doorways guarded by embedded columns.

Return back to the cross roads for a bumpy ride down to Prasonissi. It starts off through cultivation but this is quickly left behind as scrub takes over to dominate the landscape. White and pink rock-roses are common in the scrubland and, although perhaps more conspicuous down south, they thrive in all hot and dry locations. There are just three species on the island which are easily identified, see the feature box on page 156. Although the scrubland looks most hostile to more delicate plants, a few species of wild orchid also grow here but they are only to be seen in the spring as is the small yellow *Fritillaria rhodia*.

When Prasonissi comes into view, it is a sight to bring progress to a temporary halt. Here east coast and west coast are separated only by a strip of sand which leads out to the headland of Prasonissi. **Prasonissi**, or Leek Island, possibly takes its name from the wild Alliums growing there. The sand spit, which sometimes disappears under water in the storms of winter, suffers crashing walls of Aegean surf on the west side and is lapped by a gentle Mediterranean on the east. It is a great spot for windsurfers and very popular in high season.  Also in the heat of summer, the sand gets compacted enough for four wheel drives to cross over to the headland but it is best not attempted in a small saloon since rescue parties are not always on hand. Down on the beach two tavernas await and, once refreshed, the prospect of a gentle half hour stroll over the headland to see the lighthouse might  not seem so daunting.

It is another drive back up the track to rejoin the main road outside Katavia. This time turn right through the gentle, cultivated landscape towards **Agios Pavlos**. It is here that the buildings of the model farm built by the Italians can still be seen but they are now disused except for storage by local farmers. Just 3 miles (5km) on from Agios Pavlos, there is a right turn to look out for down to Plimmiri but on good road. **Plimmiri** has a huge crescent of deserted beach backed by sand dunes borrowed from some other exotic location, probably the South Pacific.

*The golden sands at Prasonissi*

*Relaxing in the sun at Prasonissi*

*A carpet of green wheat fields at Agios Pavlos*

*The huge crescent of deserted beach at Plimmiri*

# Rock-Roses

There is a view that Rhodes takes its name from the rose but these are not native to the island. Rock-roses, belonging to the *genus cistus*, are native and they thrive in the hot dry conditions found more particularly in the south. Since there are only three species growing on Rhodes, identification poses no real problems. Two are pink and the other, the sage-leaved cistus, *C. salviifolius*, is white. Separating the two pink ones is done simply on the size of the flower, *C. creticus* has the larger flower and *C. parviflorus* the smaller. Sometimes, when the two are not close for immediate comparison, and the size alone is no help then the next guide is to look at the central style. If this is equal in length to the stamens then it is *C. creticus*, if shorter it is the small flowered one.

Individually, the flowers are short lived surviving usually for only one day. The first flush of flowers in spring sees the bushes covered in bloom for a time but later in the season the flowers are much reduced in number. Often they manage to stay in flower with just one or two flowers showing until well into summer.

Herbs and plants are intertwined in the lives and culture of the Mediterranean peoples and many have their own story to tell. This is certainly true of *Cistus creticus* which has provided *gum ladanum*, highly valued in perfumery. The gum exudes from the plant and sticks to the legs and beards of goats as they graze on and amongst the bushes. One way which has been used to collect the gum is to patiently comb it from the goat's beard. The other relies on a little more help from man and was carried out by monks into the Middle Ages. A kind of leather rake was dragged over the leaves of the plant in the midday heat when the extrusion of gum takes place and the resin then gathered from the rake.

There is no village here, it is just a fishing harbour with a taverna and a small church although the construction of a new marina is supposedly in hand, as the ugly concrete mole will testify. Specialising in fish, the taverna here has a good reputation and a fine position overlooking the bay. Behind the taverna, and almost part of it, is the church which was erected on an earlier Christian basilica and incorporates some of the old pillars and marble.

For the next stop, Mesanagros, return to the main road and cross directly over to join a track. It is good stabilised track which heads inland and, after 2 miles (3km), join the surfaced road by turning left to **Mesanagros**. It is a gentle climb through undulating countryside and even when Mesanagros comes into view above there is some winding up still left before the village is reached. The road flirts with rather than penetrates the village so overshoot is a distinct possibility. Park up somewhere around the sign for O Mike's taverna. If an insistent invitation of 'come, come!' rings out on setting foot outside the car, it will be Mike himself trawling for business. He is one of those larger-than-life colourful characters so beloved of travel writers and should his invitation be accepted then no doubt he will proudly display for you his collection of English newspaper cuttings in which he is mentioned. Near to O Mike's taverna is the thirteenth-century Byzantine church of the Assumption of the Virgin Mary. If it is locked, Mike has a key and will organise someone to look after things. It is a barrel vaulted church with a pebble mosaic floor built over ruins of a fifth-century Christian basilica. Over the door is the lintel from an earlier church and inside is a painted wooden screen. Evidence around suggests it is a fair mix of ages. There are some toilets too near O Mike's taverna.

Return along the same road back to Lahania which is the last stop before setting off for home. **Lahania** was one of those villages dying on its feet until it was discovered by foreigners, mostly from Germany, and over the past decade, and even before, new residents have been buying up and restoring old property. To find the village square, unusually located at one end rather than centrally in the village, follow signs to Cafe Platanos. Shaded by a huge platanos tree, the café looks out onto two fountains and the village church. It is another village best explored on foot, particularly so as the alleyways are particularly narrow.

Leave Lahania by continuing along the surfaced road to rejoin the coast road ready for the drive north back to Rhodes Town.

## *Additional Information*

### *Accommodation*

There are no hotels in the villages so far down south of the island. There may be village rooms but it will be necessary to enquire locally. Visitors wishing to stay as near to the region as possible might consider staying in resorts south of Lindos, like Pefkos or Gennadion, in which case consult the Additional Information at the end of Chapter 4.

### *Transport*

The region is poorly served by buses and there is just one bus daily leaving Messanagros at 6.30am and calling at Katavia, Gennadion, Lardos and arriving Rhodes Town around 8.45am. It leaves Rhodes on the return run at 3pm. Arnitha too has a daily bus departing at 7am which also serves Apolakia.

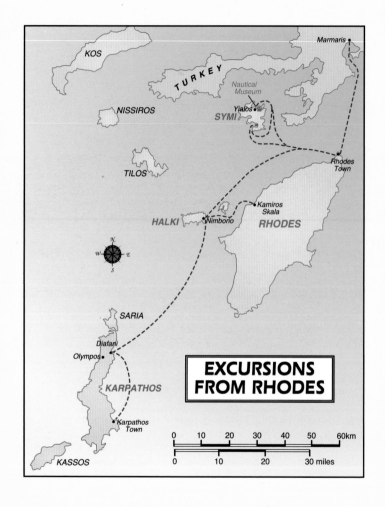

EXCURSIONS
FROM RHODES

# Excursions from Rhodes

9

Since Rhodes is well connected by air and sea, there are no end of excursions that can be planned from the island. Two of the most popular are the packaged excursions to Symi and to Marmaris in Turkey where all that is necessary is to book a ticket and turn up in time. Once at the destination the cosseting ends and many wander around waiting for the return boat totally unaware of the lost opportunities. In this chapter, some background and suggested itineraries are offered for these excursions to help fill the day profitably. Also included are two other tours, to the small island of Halki and to the larger and little visited island of Karpathos, which are easily managed from Rhodes but require a little more planning.

## Symi

**PRACTICAL DETAILS**
Symi is a small island, one of the Dodecanese group, lying 20 miles (32km) to the north-west of Rhodes close to the shores of Turkey.

Several boats leave in convoy daily from Mandraki harbour in Rhodes Town departing at 9am. All the ferry boats are of a similar size and standard except for the catamaran, *Symi II*, which is larger and faster. A ticket bought from one of the many tourist agencies is usually valid on any boat except *Symi II* which costs a little more. The journey time is a margin over 2 hours, and around 15 minutes less on the catamaran. Those intending to stay on Symi for a night or so can do so at no extra charge but must declare their intentions on entering the boat to get a return ticket.

Apart from stopping in the main harbour in Yialos, Symi's capital, all the boats also call in and spend around 1 hour at Panormitis to visit the monastery. Some boats call in the morning on the way and others call in the afternoon on the return. Those preferring to spend all the time in the main harbour on Symi should ask before boarding to find out which boats will be going directly and which will make the return directly then choose accordingly.

## THE ISLAND

Holidays have those unforgettable moments and sailing into Symi harbour is one. Elegant neo-Classical houses in ochre, yellows and gold cascade down the grey hillsides almost spilling into the indigo pool of the harbour. A clock tower guards the quay to the right where waterside tavernas spread their awnings wide denying the sun and reflecting its rays to burnish pastel houses and to brighten grey rock. Its impact is enough to hush fellow passengers leaving the tranquillity of the moment disturbed only by a chorus of clicking camera shutters!

With only a short stay in prospect there is barely time to inspect the main harbour at Yialos and visit the old village Chorio which lies above. **Yialos** is the main tourist centre where, thanks to the daily influx of visitors, all the necessary facilities can be found without travelling too far. Tavernas, restaurants, snack bars, shops and sponge sellers all crowd Mourayio, the quay where the boats dock. For centuries the Symiotes have been amongst the most brave and daring sponge fishers in the Aegean. When Suleiman the Magnificent took over the Dodecanese in 1522, Symi submitted to the Sultan and offered him a choice from the islands sponges to gain privileges which allowed them to continue their mercantile trade unhindered. A quantity of the finest sponges became the annual tax on the island. Now the best of the sponges are saved for tourists, with gentle persuasion to buy the environmentally friendly natural brown sponges instead of the clear yellow bleached variety. The environmental argument is on the lines that the chemicals used to bleach sponges afterwards become pollutants and the process actually weakens the sponge and shortens its life leading to more frequent replacement. Sponges with small

*preceding page; The elegant neo-Classical houses at Symi harbour*

pores produce a creamy lather good for babies whilst the more open sponges are better for baths and showers.

Virtually all the neo-Classical houses around the harbour are nineteenth century but there is some older architecture on view at Horio (Chorio). The island's strong association with ship building and the sea is honoured by a trireme carved in stone copied from Lindos on the Mourayio quayside and a Nautical Museum, sited at the end of the square behind the harbour, which displays models of sailing ships used in local waters, shipmakers tools, ship and diving equipment.

Bathers often swim off the rocks just around the corner from the clock tower in front of Aliki Hotel but there is a tiny beach at Nos. To find the beach, continue past Hotel Aliki and follow the paved walkway which leads very shortly to Nos where a taverna guards a small shingle beach with space for about two dozen sun beds.

There are still more tavernas across the bridge at the inner end of the harbour, which are generally quieter, and narrow streets to explore especially if shopping for groceries, souvenirs, herbs or just looking for a bar.

A little further around the quay on the side opposite Mourayio, is the taxi rank for the villages two taxis. Around here is where the minibus picks up passengers for Horio and Pedi.

**Horio**, the main village, lies up the hillside above Yialos and is reached by the Kali Strata, a stepped street which starts from the inner end of the harbour behind Captain's Hotel and Trata Taverna. Kali Strata starts modestly but soon widens to a broad street with 375 steps in short flights spaced by long slopes and with barely a shadow to protect from the heat of the midday sun. Taken at a slow pace, and provided that the roadside herb sellers do not provide a serious distraction, around 10 to 15 minutes is enough to reach the bars and taverna's at the top which mark the start of the village proper. Both the taxi and the minibus come up to the village by a longer route.

Horio is a rambling mass of houses crowded onto a saddle and divided by a confusion of narrow twisting connecting and interconnecting alleyways. Apart from the engaging ambience, the old apothecary, the museum and the old *kastro* (church) make the climb worthwhile.

From the shady pergola over the bar area at the top of Kali Strata, continue to climb but look on the right within a minute for the apothecary set back on the right. While the doctor still holds his surgery in a side room, this nineteenth-century pharmacy welcomes visitors to look around. Little has changed since the shop opened and the old porcelain jars store Nux Vomica or Tincture of Belladonna or extract of Digitalis on crowded shelves. There is also an old pressure pot for sterilisation, endless medicines and potions and a rather puzzling empty bottle of Scotch whisky!

Continue to climb the main street but notice now the blue signs on the wall for the museum which actually started right down in the harbour.

This small museum, for which entry is free, concentrates largely on the island's religious monuments. There are many of these with around one hundred barrel vaulted chapels scattered over Symi and some in quite remote places. Photographs of the oldest chapels and their frescos are shown with concise information in Greek and English including details too of some of the island's famous religious painters.

From just a little higher than the museum, signs indicate the direction of the *kastro* but lead only as far as the large church. From here cross below the church and keep in the same direction until the Kastro's walls come into view. Not too much remains now except the strong walls of this medieval fortress which was built over the old acropolis. Inside was a church dedicated to the Virgin Mary but this was destroyed in World War II and the nearby church of St George inherited its name.

Horio looks over the ridge westwards to the small water front village of **Pedi** which has the best local beach. Walking down takes around 30 minutes from George's taverna. Pedi has fishermen's cottages, waterside tavernas and some tourist accommodation loosely grouped at the sandy end of a deep inlet.

**Panormitis**, located in the extreme south-east of the island, takes around 1 hour to reach by ferry and is a highly commercialised monastery. Built in the eighteenth century and dedicated to Archangel Michael, the patron saint of Symi, Panormitis stands on the site of a smaller chapel with the same dedication which was destroyed in the Middle Ages. An imposing tiered campanile guards the entrance to a black and white pebbled courtyard. The church has fine if somewhat blackened frescos and a magnificent carved wooden iconostasis. Also there are two small museums. Alongside the church is a restaurant, accommodation and a bread shop held in high esteem by the Greeks.

# The Turkey Excursion

## PRACTICAL DETAILS

The destination of this trip is Marmaris which lies almost due north of Rhodes on the Turkish mainland. Ferry boats leave daily for this 2 hour journey but there is a faster hydrofoil service. Tickets are available from Tourist Agencies all over the island. The cost of the excursion is extraordinarily high, inflated in part by the entry tax imposed by the Turks and reciprocated by the Greeks. Normally the Greek tax is incorporated in the price but the Turkish tax has to be paid directly on entry. It is the normal procedure to collect passports for this trip the

*opposite; One of the many picturesque views overlooking Symi harbour* day before departure and return them on boarding. This excursion is not simply a change of resort, it is also a change of culture. Turkey is a Moslem country and their religious day is Friday but they follow European trading practice for trade and commerce so that Friday is normal in this respect. Saturday and Sunday are treated as weekdays and the shops are open all day so, from the point of view of planning an excursion, all days are equal. Friday, however, is market day which adds a lot of life and colour to the excursion.

For visitors who arrived in Greece on a charter flight, it is not possible to stay overnight in Turkey without breaking charter regulations. The Greeks are keen and penalise anyone who ignores these conditions by removing their return airflight ticket. This does not apply to international travellers who arrived in Greece on a scheduled flight.

## Marmaris

**Marmaris** is a major and relatively modern resort and marina on the Aegean coast of Turkey. The boat docks close to the part that was the original fishing village, now the heart of the resort, and not far from the tourist office. There is no beach immediately on hand but the nearest is at close-by Icmeler which is easily reached using the frequent mini bus (*dolmus*) service.

The site of the Friday market is inland to the west of the landing point and best located by tracking the stream of Turks carrying great bags of fruit and vegetables back to source. Lively and colourful, just about everything is for sale from mouth-watering fruit through to plastic buckets, towels, clothing and even baby chicks. Not only is the shopping good here, it is also good in Marmaris generally and many of the Greeks themselves come over just to shop. The Turks are great salesmen but sometimes their persistence upsets first time visitors. Their technique is to engage a potential customer in polite conversation then persuade them to look at their goods. A typical opening gambit is the question 'Where are you from?' and the best way to deal with this is to make no answer if no involvement is desired.

Good buys amongst the shopping includes T- shirts and clothing in general including leather goods, onyx and honey. Honey comes in a surprising number of varieties including pine, orange, cotton, eucalyptus and general flower honey. There are a number of shops which sell tiny sampler jars or will let you try some that are already open. Orange honey is very clear and light with the faintest hint of marmalade whereas the pine honey is one of the darkest with a strong flavour. Cotton and eucalyptus might seem unlikely sources but both are delicately flavoured honeys.

And, of course, there are Turkish carpets. Working on the percentage principle, considerable powers of persuasion are used to invite visitors into the salesroom. Potential customers are treated courteously and with hospitality, usually tea, orange tea or *raki*, similar to the Greek *ouzo*. The sales pitch usually covers details of the manufacture of these hand made carpets, of the plant dyes employed and the significance of the various motifs used in the designs. A range of dazzling carpets are then displayed which tempts more than a few but the salesmen remain cheerfully philosophical and just as friendly to those who leave without buying.

If shopping and wandering around the old part of town leaves time to spare, a peaceful escape needs just a short excursion out of town to **Ataturk Parki**. This lies to the east of Marmaris and is easily reached on foot in around 15 minutes by following the coast road out past the marina. This beautiful green park lying next to the sea shore is shaded by masses of *Liquidambar orientalis* trees, the same trees found in the Valley of the Butterflies on Rhodes (Chapter 6). Walkways lead on woodland strolls over rustic bridges to cafés and various picnic areas where it is not usually difficult to find some peace and quiet.

# Halki

### PRACTICAL DETAILS

Halki is a tiny island lying 10 miles (6km) off the west coast of Rhodes, just about due west of Embonas. A ferry boat provides a daily service from Halki to Kamiros Skala essentially to bring Halki residents over to Rhodes in the morning and return them in the evening. Using this service, a minimum stay of two nights needs to be spent on Halki simply to have a full day on the island. On Sunday, the ferry times make it possible to enjoy a day trip departing Kamiros Skala in the morning and returning in the evening. See the Additional Information at the end of the chapter for the actual times. One further complication is the lack of a bus service from Rhodes Town to Kamiros Skala on a Sunday which means using either a hire car or a taxi.

Ferry boats and a hydrofoil leave from Rhodes Town calling in at Halki en route to other islands but not returning the same day.

### THE ISLAND

This barren, dry, rocky island which relies on drinking water shipped over from Rhodes, is a sanctuary of peace and an idyllic escape from reality. It is almost but not quite traffic free with the few hundred residents owning just a handful of cars between them but they are hardly racing around since there is virtually nowhere to go! The port town of Nimborio grew wealthy on sponge fishing around the turn of the nineteenth and twentieth century but later many of its sponge divers emigrated to the United States, to Tarpon Springs in Florida, to set up a sponge diving community there. Fishing and sponge diving is still an important source of revenue for the island with tourism slowly making a contribution.

Landing is made at **Nimborio**, the capital and now the only settlement on the island. Here colourfully shuttered imposing mansions crowd the water front and climb the hills behind watched over disinterestedly by derelict windmills. The sight of decaying mansions and the general air of neglect apparent just a decade ago has disappeared over recent years. Once designated the island of peace and friendship supported by UNESCO, money was provided for restoration which spurred islanders to return to rebuild their own crumbling mansions. An old problem, the lack of water, has proved a mixed blessing. Development has not exceeded the bounds of restoration whilst accommodation and services are sufficient to support a small amount of tourism. Now with a handful of tavernas and a bar, and a beach nearby, Halki provides a relaxing place to unwind from the energy of modern life.

A short walk inland over the hill leads to a small sandy beach cradled in a small bay. A shady seat in the nearby taverna is the best place to watch bathers wading out far enough to swim.

High above Nimborio, out of easy reach of pirates and close to the castle, is the now deserted village of **Horio** (Chorio). Sadly, the old mule trail up to Horio has been abandoned in favour of a modern paved road (Tarpon Springs Boulevard). It is the same road which passes the beach and heads off into the hills. Around 30 to 40 minutes of early morning walking along this exposed road is sufficient to reach the crest of the hill beneath the castle. Derelict houses are spread around but the interest here is focused on the medieval castle of the Knights of St John. Head

*Halki harbour*

left from the crest up the concrete path into a churchyard and go through the gate at the side to continue upwards. Some splendid sections of the castle walls remain and inside, the derelict chapel still has some fine late Byzantine frescos. The views alone, of intricate coastlines and offshore islands, make the excursion worthwhile.

# Karpathos

## PRACTICAL DETAILS

Karpathos lies on an arc about half way between Rhodes and Crete. It is a fairly large island, the largest in the Dodecanese group after Rhodes, but under populated with only twelve villages housing some 5,000 inhabitants. Ferry boats connect Rhodes with Karpathos around twice a week but flights are much more frequent, with around four a day in summer. For visitors travelling via Athens, the most convenient programme is to include Karpathos either on the way to Rhodes or on the return journey. Travellers using the ferry service should be aware that the boats do not always run on windy days and schedules should be planned to accommodate this eventuality.

## THE ISLAND

Karpathos is a long narrow island, effectively the summit region of a submerged mountain range, lying on a north-south axis. Most of the population live in the south of the island but there is one remarkable village, Olympos, in the north which lives in isolation in its own time capsule, in an age long since past for the rest of Greece.

The island is not so easy to get around. A surfaced road links Karpathos Town (Pigadia) with the airport located on the extreme southern tip of the island and the only other surfaced road forms a southern circuit to take in the villages of Aperi, Volada, Othos, Piles, Finiki, Arkassa and Menetes. Villages further north are served by a track most suited to four-wheeled drive vehicles which penetrates the rugged, often cloud enshrouded mountains and leads all the way to Olympos.

Without industry and with little land suitable for cultivation, Karpathians have always been migrant workers and in recent years money sent home has made the island surprisingly prosperous. Since the completion of its international airport, Karpathos is turning more to tourism. One advantage of this late entry is that many of the hotels are of recent construction and even more modest C class hotels, like the Blue Bay in Karpathos Town, offer a standard of comfort and service not always found in higher class hotels on other islands.

**Karpathos Town**, the capital, hustles around a port area in the southern corner of Vrondi Bay. Tourism has managed to capture the sea front area of this busy town and filled it imaginatively with tavernas, bars and restaurants which is particularly picturesque under the evening lights. A few minutes walk to the north, is Limniati with its long stretch of sandy beach near where many hotels, including Blue Bay, are located. This is probably the best base on the island although some may prefer **Ammoopi**, 5 miles (8km) to the south which has three fine enclosed beaches but is somewhat isolated and supported only by hotels, apartments and tavernas.

The major excursion on the island is to the remote northern village of Olympos (Elymbos). It involves a boat journey to Diafani and a short bus journey up to the village itself. It is a highly packaged tour running daily but the most convenient way to enjoy Diafani and Olympos. The alternative is a lengthy drive in a four wheeled vehicle.

**Diafani**, small and colourful, is the port area for Olympos. It has a landing stage to take small boats and when larger ferries call, as some do on the run between Crete and Rhodes, passengers have to be transferred by small boat. With more than a hundred beds in hotels and rooms, Diafani attracts its own measure of tourism supported by the energies of Orfanos Travel who organise a programme of walks with drop down and pick up by boat.

Traditional costume is worn by many inhabitants, particularly by the women both here and in Olympos, for their normal daily routines. Married women wear black and single white with the single women and girls wearing more bright colours. Traditional footwear is the goatskin boot. Some of the village houses are in traditional style not dissimilar to those on Rhodes, featured on page 100, except the raised area for sleeping, here called the *soufas*, has an additional social function. When celebrations are held, such as family weddings or some religious occasion, the *soufas* is decorated with embroideries hung over the rails and transformed into the women's room where unmarried women sit and watch the celebrations taking place beneath on the floor of the house.

The journey by bus up to **Olympos** takes around 20 minutes and there are spectacular views just before arrival at the village perched on a ridge and spreading down the mountain side . The white houses, some flat roofed others with elements of neo-Classical style, are clustered together allowing streets only wide enough for mules. Although it is not the first impression, there is considerable organisation in the village plan with rows of houses following contours along the hillside with higher and lower houses accessed by steps. Tavernas and snack bars are somehow squeezed into the village as well as a hotel and pensions. There is one picture post card view not to be missed, the line of horseshoe-shaped windmills snaking out along a ridge just through the far end of the village. From here are spectacular views down the precipitous mountainside to the west coast. There are two mills still in use which grind corn for the whole village. The first mill is in the charge of a little old lady in black who is the last of her line which could eventually mean the closure of another mill. She lives in

*Karpathos Town*

*One of the fine, enclosed beaches at Ammoopi*

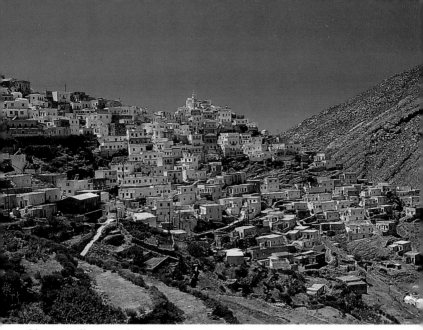

*Olympos village, perched on a ridge and spreading down the mountainside, on the island of Karpathos*

*Horseshoe-shaped windmills line a ridge at Olympos*

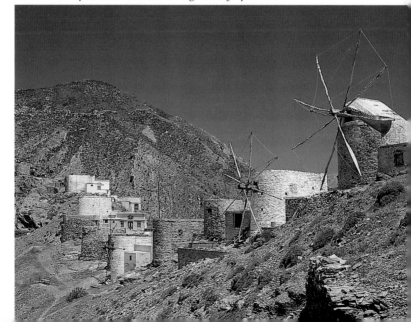

the mill for much of the year and sells a tasty, sweet pancake of thin pastry flavoured with sugar and a little spice and buying one provides the opportunity to look inside a working mill.

Much of the interest in this village centres around the way of life and the customs still observed. The origins of the village at not clearly known but thought to be from around the tenth to fifteenth century when shepherds and their families slowly gathered at one point or when the populace of a nearby village, Vroukounda, fled to the interior after destruction of their town by earthquake. Since then it has lived in virtual isolation and even its language is a unique dialect thought to maintain traces of ancient Doric and Phrygian languages. Inheritance laws are very strict and at no time are the fortunes of husband and wife ever combined but they are passed down undivided to the first born son and first born daughter. In this way, fortunes and personal power are preserved as well as some measure of population control. A second born has no inheritance, no land, no work, unless for other members of the family, and no prospects so is forced out to seek a fortune elsewhere.

The village church of Koimisis Theotokou (the Assumption of the Virgin Mary) has tiles on the floor which, until recently, belonged to certain women who had the privilege of standing there throughout the service. This tile was handed down to the eldest daughter in time. Those without tiles had to stand outside. More recently an annex has been built where men and married women can sit whilst unmarried girls sit on the balcony above.

One food speciality to try before leaving the village is *macarounes*, not dissimilar to macaroni, flavoured with cheese.

# *Additional Information*

## *Places to Visit on Symi*

### Yialos
*Nautical Museum*
Open: 10am-2pm everyday except Monday.

### Horio
*Museum of Horio*
Open: 10am-2pm everyday except Monday.

## *Accommodation on Symi*

### TELEPHONE EXCHANGE 0241

### Yialos
*Hotel Aliki* (A) Traditional house
☎ 71665

*Hotel Dorian* (A) Traditional house
☎ 71181

### Horio
*Hotel Horio* (B)
☎ 71800

*Albatross* (Cat B pension)
☎ 71707

There are many other hotels and apartments available through the following agents.

*Sunnyland Ltd*
Yialos
☎ 71413

*Opera Travel*
Yialos
☎ 72034

## Transport on Symi

There is a minibus service from Yialos to Pedi via Horio which departs from Yialos on the hour and returns from Pedi on the half hour.

## Places to Visit on Halki

**Halki**
**Horio**
*Medieval Castle*
Open site.
**Ferry Boats:**
Daily service, except Sunday, departs Halki 6am and returns from Kamiros Skala at 2.30pm.
Sunday: departs Kamiros Skala at 9am and returns from Halki at 4pm.

## Accommodation on Halki

☎ (0241) 57295 for rooms to let but there are others and apartments. Many are taken up by tour operators for the main season. It is best to enquire immediately on arrival.

## Accommodation on Karpathos

**KARPATHOS TOWN:**
**TELEPHONE EXCHANGE 0245**
**KARPATHOS (POSTAL CODE 857 00)**

*Apartments Possirama (A)*
☎ 22916-8

*Hotel Astron (B)*
☎ 22404

*Hotel Elecktra (B)*
☎ 22577

*Hotel Lymiatis (B)*
☎ 22726

*Hotel  Mediterania (B)*
☎ 22793

*Hotel Miamare (B)*
☎ 22802

*Hotel Seven Stars (B)*
☎ 22101

*Hotel Alex (C)*
☎ 22004

*Hotel Apollo (C)*
☎ 22800

*Hotel Blue Bay (C)*
☎ 22479

*Hotel Ialkos (C)*
☎ 22192

*Hotel Karpathos (C)*
☎ 22248

*Hotel Sunrise (C)*
☎ 22467

**AMMOOPI: TELEPHONE PREFIX 0245**

*Albatross (B) Hotel and Apartments*
☎ 22828

*Hotel Argo (B)*
☎ 22589

*Hotel Helios (B)*
☎ 22448

*Hotel Ammoopi Bay (C)*
☎ 22184

*Hotel Sophia (C)*
☎ 22087
For accommodation in Diafani and Olympos contact Orfanos Travel, Diafani, Karpathos ☎ 0245 51410.

## Transport on Karpathos

Local transport is not good but buses from Karpathos town serve Ammoopi (2 daily), the villages of Aperi, Volada, Othos and Piles (3 daily) and Menetes, Arkasa and Finiki (1 daily).

# 10 Fact File

# Accommodation

### Hotels

These are classified by the National Tourist Office of Greece (NTOG — EOT when in Greece.) into De Luxe, AA and A class which are subject to a minimum price structure only. Bars, restaurants and swimming pools are the facilities that you expect to find but, on a cautionary note, the class in itself is not a guarantee of the standard of service. The island has some of the finest hotels in Greece and these higher grade hotels are mostly found in the northern part of the island, especially Ixia, Rhodes Town and Faliraki, but new ones are appearing in the vicinity of Lindos.

In addition there are B, C and D classes for which maximum and minimum room rates are fixed by the NTOG. These hotels are obliged to display their category and price behind the door of each room. There is no C in the Greek alphabet so this class is represented by the gamma sign 'Γ'. Extra charges described as taxes or service may be added to the final rate and you need to check each time. Note that the charge is normally a room charge, not a charge per person and may or may not include breakfast. Room charges are seasonal with low, mid and high season rates. It is possible to bargain, especially for a stay of 3 days or more, but you are most likely to succeed when business is slack out of high season. Generally the C class hotels have rooms with bathrooms as do many of the D class but here it is not obligatory. Many of these hotels are often family run and offer a good level of cleanliness and comfort. The lower grade hotels may not have bar or restaurant facilities, except for breakfast.

### Pensions

Accommodation of this kind in small hotels or private houses can also be very good. Again, the standards are controlled and graded by the NTOG but you really need to take each one on its own merit and do not hesitate to inspect before you commit yourself. At best they are very good with private bathroom facilities and a kindly Greek family to fuss over and take care of you. At worst you keep looking around!

### Villas and Apartments

There are many scattered around popular tourist locations with some resorts, like Faliraki, having more than others. Many are in the hands of letting agencies who place them with tour operators. One technique for searching them out is to read through the holiday brochures of companies who specialise in this type of accommodation. Many of these villas are often not in use until late May so, if you

*preceding page; The Hotel Rodos Princess, Asklipion*

are around before then, it is possible to make private arrangements on the spot, sometimes at very attractive rates.

**Rooms**
In the main tourist areas, there are generally plenty of private houses offering rooms. And, if you are looking for budget accommodation, some of these will be hard to beat. If you arrive on Rhodes by ferry, the chances are that you will be met at the dockside by a dancing cluster of assorted 'Room to Let' notices, otherwise enquire at the local NTOG office or with the Tourist Police who also help in these matters.

**Camping**
Camping in areas other than on official camping grounds is not permitted in any part of the island. It is something which the Greek authorities tend to get uptight about, especially in popular tourist regions. There is now just one on Rhodes at Ladiko near Faliraki which is seasonal. The site at Lardos (near Lindos) has closed down. For details see Additional Information in Chapter 4.

# Banks

When you think of changing money, try to think of it as a morning job, especially if relying on Eurocheques. This advice will become much clearer when you study the bank opening hours which are: Monday to Thursday 8am-2pm, Friday 8am-1.30pm. Early and late season some of the outlying banks close for the winter and it may be necessary to travel into Rhodes Town.

Some of the major banks in Rhodes Town have external cash dispensers which accept leading credit cards.

Visitors with Travellers Cheques and cash should have no trouble anytime. Most hotels offer exchange facilities and there are exchange bureau in most resorts which stay open late into the night.

For those arriving in Greece via Athens, the only round the clock banking service is provided by the Agricultural Bank of Greece at East Air Terminal (International). At West Air Terminal, the National Bank of Greece is open from 7am-11am, 7 days a week.

There is a bank and post office in Rhodes airport but these only open normal business hours.

Post Offices are open only on weekdays from 7.30am-2pm. They are closed on Saturday and Sunday.

# Climate

Rhodes boasts one of the sunniest climates in Greece and from June to September the island experiences atmospheric stability with a succession of cloudless days. Temperatures rise regularly into the

30°C (80°F) and the heat is only tempered by the Meltemi wind which starts around May and blows from the north with persistent regularity. The north facing west coast takes the brunt of the wind and the east coast is more sheltered. In addition there is a daily cycle of wind throughout the summer with wind off the sea in the morning as the land heats up rapidly and the reverse after sunset when the land loses heat.

The monotonous pattern of endless days of sunshine and wind usually changes in September or sometimes a little later when depressions start to move west to east through the Mediterranean. Although the temperature falls, the weather remains warm and showers are possible and increasingly likely as autumn moves towards winter.

The cyclonic storms of winter arrive suddenly and the rain can be very heavy, causing flash floods off the mountains and filling the wide river beds. Winter continues as a mixture of heavy rain and periods of sunshine with January as the wettest month. Frost is rare and snow falls only in exceptionally hard winters.

According to the flowers, spring arrives early, as early as March but this month normally has a high number of days with rain. Spring here is as variable as anywhere in Europe. Some years March is a fine month with low rainfall, plenty of sunshine and comfortably high temperatures. In a late spring, rain showers, cool temperatures and cloudy skies persist until well into May when the transition to summer can then be almost immediate.

# Consulates

Consular help is on hand in times of emergency but this is largely in an advisory capacity. The following comments are offered in terms of guide lines only and do not fully define the powers of the office.

### Consular Help

problems over a lost passport and the issue of an emergency one if necessary.

help with problems over lost money or tickets but only by contacting relatives or friends at your request to ask them to provide the finance needed.

advise on the details of transferring funds.

encash a cheque supported by a valid banker's card but only in an emergency and as a last resort when there are no other options.

make a loan to cover repatriation expenses when this is the absolute last resort.

arrange for next of kin to be informed following an accident or death and advise on procedures.

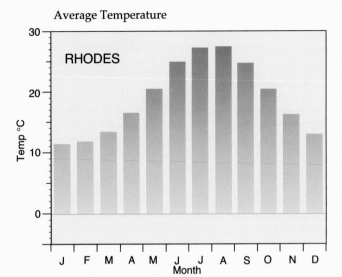

Average Temperature

RHODES

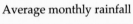

Average monthly rainfall

RHODES

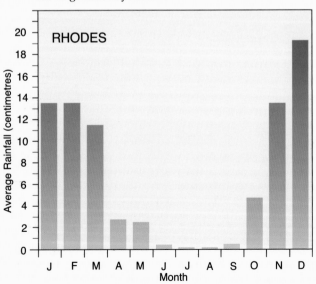

act for nationals arrested or imprisoned to inform relatives.

give guidance on organisations experienced in tracing missing people.

provide a list of local interpreters, English speaking doctors and solicitors.

They do not involve themselves in finding work or obtaining work permits. Neither will they investigate a crime, give legal advice, instigate legal procedures on your behalf or attempt to interfere with the Greek legal procedures. Nationals in hospital or imprisoned can only expect the same treatment as the Greeks and the Consul has no power to gain better conditions.

Nearest foreign Embassies and Consulates are:

**Australia**
37 D Soutsou Street &
  An Tsocha
115 21 Athens
☎ 6447303

**Canada**
4 I. Genadou Street
115 21 Athens
☎ 7239511-9

**New Zealand**
15 -17 Toscha Street
115 12 Athens
☎ 6410311-5

**UK**
Consulate
111 Amerikis Street
Rhodes
☎ 0241 27306 & 27247

**USA**
Embassy-Consulate
91 Vass. Sophias Avenue
115 21 Athens
☎ 721951-9
or contact the Voice of
America Radio Station on
Rhodes at:
Asgourou ☎ 0241 66731 or
Afandou ☎ 0241 51225

# Crime and Theft

On an island like Rhodes which receives many thousands of visitors annually, some crime and theft is inevitable. There is no need to feel threatened in any way, even throughout the evening but it is sensible to be cautious late at night, especially women on their own. Rape and muggings, unfortunately do occur but not in the quiet country areas, as might be expected, but near to the high-life night spots like the main street in Faliraki.

Many hotels have safety deposit boxes available for guests at a small charge. Otherwise, keep valuables out of sight. This is particularly true if you have a car. Cameras, personal stereos and the like are best carried with you but if you need to leave them in the car make sure they are locked in the boot.

If you are unfortunate enough to suffer a loss through theft or carelessness then report it to the Security Police, Ethalondon Street. Rhodes Town, ☎ 0241 25805. Enter through the same door as the Immigration Office and it is only open Monday to Friday. They endeavour to have English speaking staff on duty at least in the mornings so this is the best time to visit. There is a form to complete if an insurance claim is contemplated.

If your loss includes a passport then you will need to contact your Consulate on page 180.

# Currency & Credit Cards

**Money Matters**

The local currency is the *drachma* which is indicated by drx or simply Dx (ΔP) before the number. *Drachma* notes commonly in circulation include 10,000, 5000, 1000, 500, 100 and 50 with coins of 100, 50, 20, and 10 *drachma* value. The 100 and 50 *drachma* notes are steadily being replaced by coins but are still in circulation. (Avoid bringing home coins and low value notes since most banks refuse to change them).

Travellers cheques, Eurocheques and hard currencies are freely accepted at banks, Post Offices and Exchange Bureau. Credit cards and charge cards are also widely accepted in hotels, shops and restaurants especially in Rhodes Town. While most of the larger filling stations in town will accept credit cards, do not count on plastic to pay for fuel in the countryside.

Although it is possible to get a cash advance on a credit card, there still seems to be some suspicion of this transaction. Only certain banks will co-operate and the best ones to try are the National Bank of Greece and the Commercial Bank. There is a minimum size of transaction, around 15,000 *drachma*.

Always take your passport when changing money. Even though the production of a passport may not be a necessary requirement, the Greeks rely on them as a means of identification. You may even be asked for it when purchasing an internal flight ticket. The cost of changing money in terms of commission does vary and it pays to check; normally the cheapest place is at a bank and the worst place is the hotel reception.

# Disabled Facilities

Whilst there is an awareness of this problem, few practical steps have been taken to improve matters. As yet only the international hotels provide anything like adequate facilities. Outside Rhodes Town, very few places have pavements and where present they are high above the road. Presumably they are high to stop motorists parking on them. This creates a difficulty in making ramps since these descend so steeply that they are more of a danger than a help.

## Electricity

Mains electricity is supplied at 220 volts AC. Electrical equipment should be fitted with a continental two pin plug or an appropriate adapter used. A wide selection of adaptors for local plugs to interchange between two and three pin (not UK three pin) are available cheaply on the island.

## Good Beach Guide

All the best beaches on Rhodes are found down the east coast of the island. West coast visitors have to manage with narrow shingle beaches and a constant wind. The *mistral*, which blows constantly from the north throughout the summer, affects the west coast far more than the east but the beach umbrellas are set at an angle to offer sunbathers shelter. In the full heat of summer, the wind actually makes the temperatures more bearable but in early season it can be a nuisance.

### From north to south on the east coast:

**Faliraki** (Chapter 2) offers a 4 mile (6km) stretch of sandy beach. Very popular and busy, especially the central part, it is good for swimming and there is a full range of water sports and activities available from para-gliding to bungee jumping. It has just about every facility available; bars, tavernas, snacks as well as beach furniture and showers. Those who prefer things a little quieter should head for the two smaller bays at the south end.

**Ladiko** (Chapter 2) is a tiny, intimate bay with only a small sandy beach but a great atmosphere. There are a few sun beds with umbrellas and a taverna.

**Afandou** (Chapter 2) offers another enormous stretch of beach, this time largely shingle. Usually possible to find a few acres of space all to yourself. Very few facilities but there are three tavernas to the south. The sea here is always edged a milky blue.

Scenic **Tsambika** beach (Chapter 2) is the place to write your name in the sand, possibly the best on the island. Bounded by headlands and overlooked by Tsambika monastery, this bay of fine sand is a beauty spot which thankfully has not attracted the developers. It is good for swimming but there are only limited

*Tsambika beach, possibly one of the best on Rhodes*

facilities which include sun loungers and canteens. It is only accessible by car or by foot which helps to keep it from becoming too crowded.

**Agathi** beach (Chapter 3) lies just to the north of Haraki. It is an intimate and delightful stretch of sandy beach backed, unfortunately, by some unfinished developments started more than a decade ago. The gently shelving beach makes it good for children. Limited facilities in season.

**Lindos** (Chapter 3), overlooked by the Acropolis, is another beach of fine sand and of great natural beauty. It is no secret so prepare to share with a lot of other sunbathers. Good facilities and some water sports. Some doubts have been voiced about the validity of the blue flag in this enclosed bay.

**Pefkos** (Chapter 4) has some interesting if small beaches and is itself an expanding tourist development located about 10 minutes walk from the small sandy beach. Take the narrow lane at the east end of the town signposted main beach; there is a sign indicating parking too but space for 'only a few' Facilities are mostly limited to beach furnishings and snack bars. There is another small beach to the west shared with fishing boats.

*Enjoying the water sports at Lindos beach*

**Glystra** (Chapter 4) is a small sandy beach visible from the road south of Lardos. Picturesque but with limited facilities which includes sun beds.

**Plimmiri** (Chapter 8) has a large sweep of coarse sand looking like something from the South Pacific but with no facilities except a taverna.

**Prasonissi** (Chapter 8) is perched out at the very southern tip of the island and is connected only by a wide sandspit. Very picturesque with the sea approaching from both sides. To the west the sea is usually rough with breakers and to the east calm. A favourite spot for windsurfers. No facilities except for two tavernas in season.

## Greek Time

Greek normal time is 2 hours ahead of GMT. The clocks advance one hour for summertime starting the last Sunday in March and ending the last Sunday in September.

America and Canada: Greek normal time is ahead of time in America, 7 hours ahead of Eastern Standard, 8 hours ahead of Central, 9 hours ahead of mountain and 10 hours ahead of Pacific Time.

Australia and New Zealand; Greek normal time is 7½ hours behind South Australia, 8 hours behind New South Wales, Tasmania and Victoria and 10 hours behind time in New Zealand. These differences relate to GMT but, to take into account clock changes for Daylight Saving hours, the following corrections should be made: add 1 hour to these differences from late September to the end of March and subtract 1 hour from late March to the end of September.

## Health Care

For minor ailments like headaches, mosquito bites or tummy upsets, head for the chemist shop (*farmakion*). If you need a further supply of prescription drugs make sure to take a copy of your prescription and the chances are that you will be able to get them, and cheaply too. Pharmacies are open normal shop hours and most seem to speak English. Certain chemist shops are on rota to provide a 24 hour service and information for the nearest is posted in the pharmacy window.

If it is a doctor or dentist you require, the chemist shop should again be able to assist. If that does not work then contact the Tourist Police. There are plenty of English speaking doctors and dentists on Rhodes.

Problems really start if hospital treatment is required. European countries have reciprocal arrangements with Greece for free medical treatment, subject to certain restrictions. For this reason British visitors should take an E111 form obtained from the Post Office. The story does not end there. To operate the scheme you need to find the local Greek Social Insurance office (IKA) who, after inspecting your E111, will direct you to a registered doctor or dentist. If you are in a region remote from the IKA office which is in Rhodes Town then you must pay privately for your treatment and present your bills to an IKA official before you leave Rhodes. Up to half your costs may be refunded. The best answer is to ensure that you have adequate holiday insurance cover.

Emergency treatment, sunburn, broken bones etc, is free in state hospitals. The situation is less happy if you require treatment as an in-patient. In many of these hospitals, nursing care is restricted only to medical treatment and it is left to the family to supply general nursing care, drinks, food and even blankets. It is generally preferable to activate private medical insurance.

# Health Hazards

Some of the more obvious ones can be avoided with a little care. Sunburn and sunstroke fall into this category. The sun is very burning even on a hazy day, particularly on Rhodes, so great care is needed in protecting yourself, especially at the start of your holiday. Crawling beneath a parasol is not necessarily the full answer since the sun's rays reflect to some extent from the sand. Avoid, if possible, sunbathing in the middle of the day, from 10am-2pm when the sun it at its highest and most direct. Sun creams help considerably but, at least for the first few days, take some very light clothing to cover up and control the exposure of your skin to the sun. A slowly acquired tan lasts longer.

Even mild sunburn can be painful and may cause a chill feeling but if fever, vomiting or blistering occurs then professional help is essential.

Mosquitoes feed most actively at dusk and dawn but they can still be a nuisance throughout the evening and the night. If you sit or dine outside in the evening, particularly near trees, either cover up your arms and legs or use insect repellent. An electric machine which slowly vaporises a pellet is very efficient, especially in a closed room and there are sprays available for more instant results if intruders are spotted. Anthisan cream is an effective treatment for bites, particularly if applied immediately.

Care is needed on the beach to avoid stings from jelly fish and, in rocky regions, from sea urchins. If you are unlucky enough to have a brush with the latter then it is important to ensure that all the spines are properly removed. Wearing beach shoes will give your feet some protection from stings of this nature.

Stomach upsets are perhaps the most common ailment. The excess olive oil used in cooking and over salads can be a cause of this so take care with oily foods, at least to start with. The digestive system adjusts to this within a few days and you can soon eat giant beans swimming in oil without fear. Squeeze plenty of fresh lemon over your food to counter the oil and, if still troubled, an acidic drink, like Coca-Cola, helps to settle things. Drinking wine to excess can cause similar symptoms too. More serious are the upsets caused by bad water and bad food. Generally the water on Rhodes is safe to drink but in high summer it pays to be more careful and use bottled water which is freely available. Avoiding food poisoning is not always possible but there are elementary precautions that can help. Most tavernas prepare cooked dishes for the lunch time trade and these are left keeping warm until finally sold. If they are still there in the evening, and they often are, avoid them. Ask for something which will require grilling or roasting.

# Holiday Insurance

Whichever holiday insurance you choose, make sure that the cover for medical expenses is more than adequate. It helps too if there is an emergency 24 hour contact to take care of arrangements, including repatriation if necessary. Injuries caused whilst taking part in certain hazardous pursuits are normally excluded from medical cover. Look carefully at the specified hazardous pursuits; in recent times, injuries caused by riding a moped or motor-bike have been added to the list by some insurers.

# Language

Many Greeks speak good English, especially in tourist areas. Children learn it in state schools and most of them attend private schools as well. After all, English is the official second language in Greece and all official notices are presented in Greek and English, at least the more recent notices. Therein lies the danger. It is all too easy to expect and rely on every Greek to speak English which is clearly not the case when you move into country areas.

Some knowledge of the Greek language is not only useful to help you get by, but can enhance enormously the pleasure of your holiday. The Rhodians really warm to you if you make the slightest effort with their language. Do not worry about perfection in pronunciation in the beginning, just give it a go. The Greeks are very outgoing and, if they have any English, they will try it out no matter how fractured it is. Take a leaf from their book. As long as you make an effort, the Greeks will love you for it and once you can string a few words together you might find their hospitality overwhelming.

Perhaps the biggest hurdle to getting started is the Greek alphabet itself. If you take a little time to study it, you will find it is not really so different. Isolate the letters which are unique to the Greek alphabet and the remainder generally follow the sequence of the English alphabet. The language is phonetic so time taken over learning the sounds of the letters will be well rewarded in subsequent progress. Two pieces of advice to get you started on the right foot. (1) Treat all vowels equally and do not attempt to lengthen them. (2) Avoid breaking a word down into syllables as in English, instead, follow the stress pattern indicated by the accent in the word.

### Place Names
With no official transliteration, the latinisation of the Greek alphabet is open to various interpretations which leads to much confusion. The conversion of the double consonants, for example, is one cause of difficulty. The Greek **nt** is pronounced as **d** at the start of a

word but **nd** in the middle. A Greek word starting with **nt** is almost invariably Latinised to begin with **d** but in the middle of the word both **nt** and **nd** can be observed. Afandou on Rhodes appears on some maps as Afantou. Vowel sounds, especially **e** and **i**, do not always strictly correspond so there is a tendency to substitute the more phonetically correct. Some single consonants have no strict equivalent either, such as X, pronounced as the **ch** in loch, and this is Latinised to **ch**, which is a mile away phonetically, or **h** which is a little better. The village of Xora appears as Chora or Hora. All these difficulties are reflected in the spelling of place names. Pick up three different maps and it is more than likely that many of the same villages will have three different spellings. The philosophy adopted for this book is firstly to follow the spelling observed on the sign outside the village or, since many villages are without name boards, use the spelling which leads to a more accurate pronunciation. With a number of Greek islands, the English name is not the same as the Greek name and may bear no relationship, Corfu, for example is the English name for Kerkyra. With Rhodes the difference is not so marked but the Rhodians like to hear their name, Rodos, used where possible.

## Luggage

Since Greece is a full member of the EU, it is very likely that, should you forget your favourite brand of toothpaste, you will be able to buy it in the shops there. All leading brands of food and products are freely available, give or take some national peculiarities. Brands of tea and breakfast cereal fall into this category. The Greeks do not normally start the day with breakfast instead they nibble the morning away with their own versions of fast food, cheese pies (*tiropitta*) and *souvlaki* in pitta bread are well favoured. However, a limited range of breakfast cereals can be bought in most tourist regions. With tea it is a little easier, if you have a favourite brand of tea or tea bags then it is easy to find room for some in your luggage. There are a few other items which are worth considering if only to save time shopping when you are there:

A universal sink plug — not so essential but always worth having when travelling.

An electric mosquito repeller and tablets _ these are readily available in Greece but small 'travel' types are freely available which are a convenient size for packing and will last for years. Make sure you buy one with a continental 2 pin plug.

Insect repellent - if you prefer a particular brand, buy it at home.

Two other useful items are a compact folding umbrella, particularly if you are visiting Rhodes outside the main season. Rain showers tend to be short and, with the rain falling straight down, an umbrella gives good protection, better than a waterproof which can quickly make you hot and sweaty. An umbrella also makes an excellent sunshade. A small rucksack is useful too, not just for if you go walking, but for general use when heading for the beach or off on a shopping trip. Walkers might consider taking a plastic water bottle. It is important to carry water when walking in a hot climate and it is difficult to buy a plastic bottle in Greece which does not leak into your rucksack! The same advice is offered to motorists too. Unless you live in a hot climate, it is sometimes hard to appreciate the constant need to drink and how that need is best supplied by nothing other than water. Simply having water on hand when needed can add a lot to your comfort level and enjoyment of the excursion.

It is rarely necessary to take a heavy jumper but it is always useful to take some thinner layers of clothing which you can wear together. Sometimes it is cool in the evening or you may feel cool after the heat of the sun. If you intend to do any serious walking, on country tracks as opposed to city streets, make sure you have suitable footwear.

Most basic medical requirements, plasters, bandages, headache pills can be bought in chemist shops on Rhodes. More than that, many drugs normally available in Britain only on prescription can be bought over the counter on demand and at reasonable prices.

Note that codeine and drugs containing codeine are strictly banned in Greece so be sure to exclude these from your luggage.

## Maps

Even with a good sense of humour, you are unlikely to get too many laughs from a road map of Rhodes. In the main they look good but accuracy is something they are careful to avoid, or so the cynics say. The main roads are reliably marked but the position of joining roads does not necessarily relate to reality, a few roads commonly shown on maps do not exist and a number of roads built in the last decade have not yet been mapped. Generally, the signposting is fairly good on Rhodes with the Greek signs displayed first with the Latinised version a little nearer the junction. The most reliable maps are the ones shown throughout the chapters of this book.

## Newspapers & Magazines

The *Financial Time*s, most British newspapers, a selection from European countries and the *Herald Tribune* are usually available in Rhodes City and centres of tourism. Mostly they are one day late and sometimes more. Expect a fair mark up in price. The place to look for newspapers is in the tourist shops, supermarkets and at the kiosks (*periptera*) where you will see them displayed on racks or along the counter.

Also available in Rhodes Town on the day of issue is *Athens News*, published in the English language. It contains a mix of local and international stories but the entertainment section announcing events and concerts relates only to Athens. The English language is constantly being pushed into areas where no man has dared before but, notwithstanding, it gives an interesting insight into Greek attitudes. By far the best local paper, and free, is the *Rodos News*. Focused clearly on the island, it is packed with useful information on local events, history, news and travel timetables. Look for it in the Tourist Office and many other shops on the island, especially travel agents. It is produced on a monthly schedule throughout the tourist season. A selection of English and European magazines is also available.

## Nudism

Topless bathing is commonplace on all public beaches on Rhodes. Nude bathing is not acceptable but is practised with discretion on some of the more remote and secluded beaches although these are increasingly difficult to find.

## Passports & Visas

EU nationals should not require a passport but still do.

Nationals from America, Australia, Canada, New Zealand, Norway, Sweden, Finland and certain other nations require only a valid passport for a stay of up to 3 months in Greece. For a stay exceeding 3 months, it is necessary to register at the Immigration Department, Ethalondon Street Rhodes Town, ☎ 0241 25805. The whole process is long and drawn out, often requiring 2 to 3 weeks or more, and you will be asked to provide up to 6 passport size photographs. Worth taking with you if a long stay is planned. In addition you will be asked to show visible means of support, ie a good number of money exchange slips. If convenient, one option is to leave the country briefly, preferably overnight, and return making sure that you get a passport stamp on re-entry. Alternatively, plead ignorance of the requirements and opt to pay the fine when you leave the country which is quite small, roughly equalling the duties you would have paid for an extended visa.

## Pets

Cats and dogs require health and rabies inoculation certificates issued by a veterinary authority in the country of origin not more than 12 months (cats 6 months) and not less than 6 days prior to arrival.

## Photography

Signs which show a picture of a camera crossed out indicate a prohibited area for photography. Notices of this kind are posted near every military establishment, no matter how small or insignificant. Disregard this at your peril. The Greeks are still paranoiac about security and anyone found using a camera in a prohibited zone faces unpleasant consequences. The photographer is normally held in custody whilst the film is developed and inspected. It could mean overnight detention.

Photography on archaeological sites is free but if you wish to use a tripod without the insertion of a live subject then a fee is demanded.

Photography with a camera mounted on a tripod is prohibited in museums as is the use of flash in some. Video cameras are often subject to a fee.

Outdoors, the light for photography is brilliant. Summer haze can cause difficulties with distant shots but the use of a UV or Skylight filter is helpful here. Some of the clearest days occur in spring when a cool north wind blows. Midday light is harsh and contrasty, mornings and evening provide the best lighting conditions for serious photography.

## Places to Visit

### Ancient Sites and Monasteries

Most of the ancient sites are fenced off and there is an entrance fee to look around. Generally they are free to all on Sunday and closed on Monday. Opening and closing times have been regularised and these can be found either in the text or at the end of the appropriate chapter. Monasteries are often closed in the afternoon so, as a general guide, it is best to plan a morning visit. Do not count on being able to buy site guides at all sites, sometimes only glossy books are sold. If your interest runs deeper than the information given in the chapters of this book, the best advice is to go equipped with your own guide. Students can claim reduced fees on production of a student's card.

Archaeological sites are closed on certain public holidays which include 1 January, 25 March, Good Friday and Easter Monday, 1 May and 25 and 26 December.

## Museums

Here again there is a charge for admission and all close on a Monday. Refer to the end of the appropriate chapter for further details.

The museums too are closed, or open only for a short while, on the public holidays listed under ancient sites. In addition they have half-days on Shrove Monday, Whitsunday, 15 August, 28 October and Epiphany, 6 January.

# Postal Services

Post Offices open on weekdays from 7.30am-2pm. They are closed on Saturday and Sunday.

Stamps (*grammatosima*) can be purchased at the Post Office, sometimes at a special counter, or at a kiosk (*periptero*). They are also available in many shops and some of the larger hotels but at a slightly increased price.

Letters from Greece to overseas destinations are delivered fairly speedily, 4 to 6 days for Europe, 6 to 8 for America and longer for Australia and New Zealand. For a speedier delivery, ask for express post on which there is a fairly modest surcharge but it cuts 2 to 3 days off the delivery time.

Post cards take forever, or so it seems, especially at peak holiday times. Even to nearby Europe they regularly take 2 weeks which often means you have reached home before the cards you sent. Cards go at the same postal rate as letters so one technique is to slip a card inside an airmail envelope and have it treated as a letter. It leaves more space on the card for writing too. Envelopes (*fakellos*) can be bought very cheaply at stationers.

Anyone staying long enough to receive mail can use Poste Restante. This system works fairly well in Rhodes City. The letter should be clearly addressed and marked Poste Restante; be sure that your name is clearly printed. Some identification will be required, usually passport, when you collect your letter. Letters are held for one month.

Postcodes on the island vary with the town. Some of the major resorts are listed below:

Rhodes Town 851 00
Ixia & Trianda 851 01
Faliraki 851 02
Lindos 851 07

A telegram, telex or fax can be sent from the Telecommunications Office (OTE).

# Public Holidays and Festivals

The Greek calendar overflows with red letter days; public holidays, Saints days and festivals. On public holidays, banks, shops and offices are closed although restaurants and tavernas normally stay open. Public transport is often interrupted too, reverting either to a Sunday service or to none at all. Filling stations also close for many of the holidays. The days to watch out for are:

1 January — New Year's Day
6 January — Epiphany
7 March — Rhodes Independence Day
25 March — Greek Independence Day;
Monday before Lent — Clean Monday
April — Good Friday & Easter Monday
1 May — May Day
15 August — Assumption of the Blessed Virgin Mary
28 October — 'Ochi' Day
25 December — Christmas Day
26 December — Boxing Day

Easter is variable and does not always coincide with Easter throughout the rest of Europe.

Name-days are one reason why the calendar is so full of celebrations. It has been a long tradition for Greeks to ignore birthdays to celebrate instead the special day of their saint, and there are a lot of saints. If you see people wandering around with cake boxes neatly tied with fancy ribbon, or bunches of flowers or unusual activity around one of the many churches, then the chances are that it is a name day. The custom is for the person celebrating to offer hospitality to friends, to neighbours and to almost anyone who will partake of a little *ouzo* and refreshments.

Some of the big name days to watch out for are:

23 April — St George's day; all Georges everywhere celebrate their special day but in addition it is also the national day of Greece.
21 May — Saints Konstantinos and Eleni.
29 June — St Peter and St Paul
15 August — Assumption of the Blessed Virgin Mary. This is the day when millions of Marias celebrate and an important day in the religious calendar often marked by local pilgrimages or festivals.
8 November — for all Michaels and Gabriels.
6 December — the feast of St Nicholas.

Easter is the biggest and the most important celebration of the year. The arrival of Carnival time starts the long build up. This festival takes place throughout the 3 weeks before Lent and may commence as early as late January. Fancy dress is an important part of the tradition throughout the whole of Greece. It arises from the period of Turkish occupation when the Greeks were banned from conducting these celebrations. Driven under cover, festivities continued with people disguised to prevent recognition. Now it is firmly rooted into the custom and fancy dress and costumes are worn at all events. The children wander the streets in fancy dress and traditionally show defiance by wearing their disguises on the last school day of Carnival.

All this comes to an abrupt end with a complete change of mood on 'Clean Monday' (Kathari Deutera), the Monday before Lent. This is a public holiday when families traditionally exodus to the country to fly kites and to picnic, which mostly means heading to a taverna. Special meat-free menus are the order of the day.

It is back to the quiet life throughout Lent which is still strictly observed by many, especially in country regions. Serious preparations for Easter start on Maundy Thursday. How hens are persuaded to lay so actively for the occasion remains a mystery but shoppers are out buying eggs, not by the tens but by the hundreds. The rest of the day is spent in boiling the eggs and dying them red in the process. The colour red is supposed to have protective powers and the first egg dyed belongs to the Virgin.

Good Friday is a day of complete fast and widely observed. In tourist regions tavernas are open and life goes on as normal but in country areas it can be difficult or impossible to find food. Yellow or brown 'impure' candles are on sale everywhere ready for the evening church service. The sombre mood of the day is heightened by the continual tolling of church bells. It is a day for remembering their own dead; graves are visited and wreaths are laid. In the evening, the burial of Christ is the most moving and widely attended service in the whole of the Greek Orthodox calendar. The Epitaphios, the funeral bier of Christ, is centre stage in the services which start around 9pm. Garlanded with fresh flowers and with a gilded canopy, the Epitaphios bearing the coffin of Christ is ceremoniously taken from church in dignified candle-lit procession followed by silent mourners. The processions from all the local churches meet in the town square for a further short service. This is the most poignant moment of the evening, cafés close, tavernas close and there is not one Greek who would willingly miss it. The processions return slowly to their churches, stopping at each street corner for a short prayer.

Saturday brings an air of expectancy. Gone are the yellow candles; white candles are being eagerly bought ready for the evening service. Funereal drapes are removed in the churches and decorations of laurel and myrtle take their place. In dimly lit churches everywhere, services begin. Slowly the light intensity increases reaching full brightness at midnight when priests triumphantly chant 'Christ is risen' (Christos anesti). The sanctuary doors open to show that the Epitaphios is empty. Light from the priest's candle is passed to the congregation and that flame is rapidly passed from candle to candle until it reaches the waiting crowds outside. Fire crackers drown the clamour of the church bells as the crowd erupts in joyous celebration and greetings of 'Christos anesti' ring out loudest of all. The crowds disperse shortly carefully protecting their burning candle; it is a good omen to enter the home with the flame still burning and make a sooty sign of the cross on the door lintel.

Sunday is a day of out and out rejoicing. The big occasion of the day is roasting the lamb or goat. On Rhodes oven roasting is traditional but spit roasting is also popular. Charcoal fires are lit early in the morning and the spit roasting is done with loving care over some 5 hours with copious quantities of *ouzo* or *retsina* to help things along. All those red eggs now appear and are used in friendly competition. Each contestant taps their egg hard enough to break an opponent's but not their own.

Easter Monday has no special ceremonies or rituals and passes as any normal public holiday.

### Cultural Events
In addition to the major festivals listed with each chapter, religious fairs, *panayiria*, are commonplace in the summer months. *Panayiria* are a celebration of the name day of a particular church or monastery and usually held in the vicinity of the establishment. Celebrations are colourful, often beginning on the eve of the name day and continue throughout the actual day. Eating, drinking and dancing are central to any celebration for the Greeks so the barbecue is certain to be in operation. When the crowds are big enough, the vendors join in selling just about anything, baubles, bangles and beads.

A word of warning too. Each town and village has its own saint's day and sometimes, depending on the local whim and the phase of the moon, a holiday is called. This decision is often not taken until the day before so there is no way you can plan for such eventualities.

# Public Toilets

The most usual sign is WC with figures to indicate ladies (*gynaikon*) and gents (*andron*). Toilets in Rhodes Town are surprisingly good and usually free, certainly above the standard normally found in

Greece. There are also toilets in museums and at archaeological sites which are also good. Toilet paper is sometimes supplied where there is an attendant and very occasionally elsewhere. Take your own supply.

# Public Transport

### Buses

There are two bus stations in Rhodes situated close together behind the new market. The East Side bus station is in Rimini Square (outside the Sound and Light Theatre) and buses from here serve the towns and villages on the east side of the island. The West Side bus station is located in Averof Street (adjoining new market) and serves the Ixia, Trianda side of the island. All these buses have a conductor aboard to collect fairs. Buses can and do get overcrowded but rarely reject passengers unless it is physically impossible to get another one aboard. Printed timetables are usually available from the Tourist Office and are included in the *Rodos News* free paper. The frequency of services is much less in winter but builds up as the tourist season gets underway. Throughout May the timetable changes weekly until the service reaches its maximum frequency sometime in June which is then held until early September. The timetable holds equally from Monday through to Saturday but Sunday sees a reduction in the number of buses to about half.

The buses depart Rhodes Town strictly on schedule and sometimes a fraction early. Intermediate times depend on traffic conditions but on quieter days, particularly Sundays, it pays to be at the stop early.

Buses from East Side which are at least hourly and often more frequent serve the following destinations:

**Faliraki** for which the Kalithies bus is also suitable, passing along the main road but not actually going into the resort.

**Lindos**: this bus also passes Faliraki and calls in at Afandou, Archangelos and some divert through Malona and Massari.

The West Side station has a frequent service, virtually half hourly all day long, to the airport which is also convenient for Ixia, Trianda and Paradission.

**Koskinou**, which is on the eastern side of the island, is served from the West Side station.

There are also local town buses which run half hourly and connect Rhodes Town with its close suburbs. These start from Mandraki harbour and a fixed price ticket must be purchased from the ticket office by the bus station before boarding. Two of the buses in particular are useful to visitors, the N3 to Rodini Park and the N5 to Monte Smith.

**Taxis**

Taxis are relatively cheap and well used on Rhodes. All licensed taxis are designated by a roof sign and fitted with a meter which displays the fare in *drachmas*. The rate of charges and surcharges are all fixed. Within the city boundaries taxi fares are charged at the single rate and you may see 1 displayed in a solitary box on the meter. Once you travel outside the city boundary, the double rate applies so it is likely you will see the driver alter the meter so that 2 shows in the box. Legitimate small surcharges are allowed for a sizeable piece of luggage, for attending an airport, port or station for the benefit of passengers, and for late night or very early morning travel. Surcharges are permitted too at holiday times, especially Christmas and Easter. Picking up a second fare is allowed too so you may find yourself sharing a taxi.

Most of the licensed taxi drivers are good and honest but there are always a few around who regard tourists as a good source of revenue. Some of the tricks encountered include; the meter does not work, the meter set on the double rate when it should be single and, worst of all, multiplying the charge by ten which is easily done by wrongly reading the display on the modern digital meter.

If you intend to travel a distance, it is common practice to negotiate your fare with the driver before you start the journey. Do not hesitate to ask two or three drivers for a quote on the fare, it is the only yardstick available.

Radio Taxis (☎ 0241 64712) offer a 24 hour service island-wide otherwise, there are taxi ranks in:

Rhodes Town
Faliraki
Archangelos
Lindos ☎ 0244 34166
Lardos ☎ 0244 44047
Gennadion ☎ 0244 43313

As usual, if there are no taxis at the rank the telephone will be unanswered. One last word of warning, taxis are sometimes scarce on Sundays, Bank, Public and religious holidays.

# Shopping

Regulations on opening hours have changed recently to adjust to market needs. Different regions have their own views on this so there is now greater confusion than ever over opening times. Big supermarkets and department stores open: Monday to Friday 8am-8pm. Saturday 8am-3pm.

Pharmacies: Monday and Wednesday 8am-2.30pm. Tuesday, Thursday and Friday 8am-2pm and 5pm-8pm.

There is also a duty rosta for pharmacies so that at least one in the vicinity is open on Saturday and Sunday. Usually a note on the door of the pharmacy details the duty chemist. The opening hours for pharmacies are fairly typical of the opening hours in small towns and villages. They argue, with some justification, everybody wants to sleep in the afternoon and nobody wants to shop.

In tourist areas, shopping hours are much more relaxed. Tourist shops in particular are open all day long but supermarkets, butchers, bakers and the like tend to observe more restricted hours.

The *periptero*, the cornerstone of Greek society, is open all day long and from there you can buy anything from chocolate to ice creams, soap to postage stamps and road maps to matches.

# Sports & Pastimes

### Water Sports
Recent years have seen a big increase in the popularity of wind surfing. Many of the small bays and coves are ideally suited to this sport and boards can be hired in most holiday resorts. Favoured spots for the experts are the west coast with its constant wind in summer and down at Prasonissi at the southern tip of the island. Lessons for beginners are generally available too at rates which are still very reasonable.

Water-skiing is available at many of the larger resorts as well as parascending.

Scuba diving is strictly prohibited unless in the control of a recognised diving school and only in designated areas. With so many antiquities in the waters around Rhodes, it is forbidden to remove anything from the sea bed and infringements normally result in a prison sentence. Two diving schools on Rhodes, Waterhoppers Diving School (☎ 0241 76178) and Dive Med Centre (☎ 0241 33654) both run courses for all levels from novices looking for a one off experience through to training for qualifications.

### Tennis
Courts are mostly to be found in the better class hotels but some allow non residents to use the facilities for a charge.

### Golf
The 18-hole course at Afandou is the one and only course on the island.

### Horse-riding
Horse-riding is available for visitors at two centres, one between Ialysos and Filerimos and the other between Asgourou and Faliraki.

**Walking**

Rhodes provides abundant opportunities for hill and coastal walking and there is a guide book specifically geared towards this activity although a number of short walks are detailed throughout the pages of this book.

**Yachting**

Rhodes, a port of entry, is ideally positioned for those who wish to explore the area by sea and has a well equipped modern marina at Mandraki harbour (☎ 0241 27690). There is no size limit on boats and the facilities available include electricity, water, repairs, 40 ton hoist, slipway, diesel and fuel gardiennage and chandlery. Mooring fees are available on application. Entrance to the harbour can be dangerous in strong east to south-east winds. British Admiralty charts are available from Yacht Agency Rhodes International Ltd who also hire out craft, crewed or bareboat, sail or power (☎ 0241 30504/5).

# Telephone Services

The cheapest place to make telephone calls is from the Telecommunications office, the OTE. In Rhodes Town this is situated on 25 Martiou Street. Look for a building with a large telecommunications dish and aerials on top, and head for that. Inside the OTE there are a range of telephone booths, each one numbered. Ask at the counter for a token and use the booth of the same number. The call meter is set on the wall above the telephone and this should be set to zero. If not, hang out of the booth and attract the attention of the counter clerk who will reset it. Only when it is on zero can you actually make a call. The ringing tone for an international call will be unfamiliar and depends on the destination country. An engaged tone is mostly a series of rapid bleeps. Throughout the call you can see the meter which usually displays the charge directly in *drachmas*. When the call is finished head to the counter and declare your booth number and pay. Faliraki too has a small OTE in a yellow van on the sea front which operates only in the main holiday season.

Most telephone booths on the island have now been converted to card phones and these too are convenient and economical. Cards, loaded with 100 units, are available often from the shop or *periptero* nearest the booth and the cost per unit is exactly the same as the OTE charge. The advantage of the OTE is that payment is made only for the units used whereas a card may be more units than required.

Many *periptera*, the small kiosks which sell just about everything, have metered phones for public use. Some, but not all, will allow their use for international calls. These are useful in quiet locations but in a busy thoroughfare you have to compete with all the noise and bustle. The rate per call unit is not advertised so you will need to ask and the meter is often not displayed so you must rely on the vendors word for the number of units used.

In the main holiday resorts a number of the tourist agencies offer a telephone service and often call themselves telephone exchanges. Although sometimes convenient, they are run for profit so expect to pay a higher rate.

Hotels have telephones for use by residents, mostly in the rooms but sometimes at reception. They charge a much higher rate per unit so it pays to ascertain the hotel rate and compare with the rate at the OTE.

International dialling codes from Greece are as follows: UK & Northern Ireland 0044: United States & Canada 001: Australia 0061: New Zealand: 0064.

The exchange numbers for Rhodes cover three sectors. The north (0241) covers Rhodes Town roughly down to a line across between Soroni and Afandou. The south-west (0246) covering Embonas, Salakos, Monolithos and Apolakia and the south-east (0244) for Archangelos, Lindos, Lardos, Gennadion and Katavia.

Other area codes include: Athens 01; Thessaloniki 031; Kos, Nissiros, Astipalea 0242; Kalymnos 0243; Karpathos, Kassos 0245; Leros, Lipsi, Patmos 0247.

# Tipping

There are no hard and fast rules on tipping. Normally, the Greeks simply leave behind the small change after a meal and perhaps the best guide is to reward only for good service in a restaurant. Taxi drivers expect a tip as does the chamber maid in the hotel otherwise it is entirely by discretion.

# Tourist Information Centres

The main Greek National Tourist Office is located in Rhodes Town at 5 Makariou and Papagou Streets and there is a temporary high season office in Rimini Square near the bus station. There is also an information office in Lindos.

# Travelling to Rhodes

## By Air

The easiest, cheapest and quickest way is to take a charter flight from Britain directly to the island. There are many from airports all over the country throughout the holiday season. If travelling out of season or from America or Canada, the route is via Athens which may or may not require an overnight stop depending on arrival times. Olympic Airways handle the ongoing flights between Athens and Rhodes and it is usually possible to book this flight at the same time as the main flight. New flight operators, SEEA and Air Greece, are now starting to operate flights between Athens and the major islands and offer more competitive rates.

There are two airports in Athens, the West Terminal which operates Olympic Airways flights both internal and international, and the East Terminal which handles international flights by all other carriers. Although these two terminals lie within the same complex and use the same runways, it is a lengthy journey around the perimeter to change from one to the other. The connecting bus service is often of limited frequency and the bulk of the transfers are made by taxi. When faced with the ongoing journey to Rhodes, using Olympic Airways for the whole journey avoids the inconvenience of changing airports.

For travellers faced with an overnight stop in Athens, there is a hotel reservation desk within the terminal building and airline buses operate a regular service into the city centre.

**By Car**
Routes by car all centre on Athens. From here there are daily car ferries to Rhodes.

# Travelling on Rhodes

Driving on Rhodes is on the right hand side of the road and overtaking on the left. In the event of an accident where the driver was proven to be on the wrong side of the road, the insurance is invalidated. Unless there are signs indicating otherwise, the speed limits are as follows: built-up areas 50kph (31mph), outside built-up areas 80kph (50mph).

Traffic moving along main roads outside towns has priority at intersections; in towns give way to traffic from the right. On approaching and on roundabouts, vehicles must give way to traffic coming from the right.

Unleaded fuel (*amolivthi venzini*) is freely available on Rhodes but not always in the country areas or the southern villages. The two grades of fuel (*venzini*) normally on offer are Apli at 91/92 octane which has now largely been replaced by unleaded and Super at 96/98 octane. Diesel is also widely available and, like fuel, is sold by the litre. Hire car users are required to use Super if not an unleaded or diesel vehicle.

Parking in Rhodes Town is something of a problem although there are large car parks on the front just north of the entrance to Mandraki harbour. These tend to fill early and often the best solution is to leave the car in the suburbs and walk.

There are plenty of parking restrictions, often ignored by the

Greeks but illegal parking can result in a ticket and a hefty fine. The ticket indicates the amount of the fine and where and when to pay it. The police are not empowered to collect on the spot fines. Vehicular access to the old town is prohibited to non residents.

With one of the worst accident rates in Europe, driving in Greece demands a cautious attitude from the onset. The discipline shown by the majority of drivers in Western European countries, which brings order to traffic flow, is often missing from Greek drivers but the Rhodian drivers are a little more orderly. Drive with your own safety in mind. Another major hazard is the state of the roads. Pot holes are a serious danger and can be encountered unexpectedly even on well surfaced roads. Some of the holes are large enough to cause damage to tyres and wheels. A line of rocks on the road guiding you towards the centre is the usual warning of edge subsidence and there will often be no other warning signs. Minor roads, which are well surfaced, may suddenly become unmetalled. Road works may have no hazard warning signs or irregular ones such as a pile of earth or a milk crate with a small flag.

Passenger cars, trailers, motorcycles and sidecars can be cleared through Customs for use for 4 months (extendible) if the owner is the holder of a corresponding 'Carnet de Passage en Douane' issued by the automobile and touring clubs of his country of origin. In the absence of such a document, motor vehicles are admitted temporarily without payment of import duty or tax by making an entry on the owner's passport whereupon a free use card is issued by Customs.

Tourists from North America, Australia and South Africa have the right to use their automobiles for 2 years upon approval by the appropriate Customs Authority. Road taxes are paid for the second year.

Motorists from EU countries and Austria need only a valid driving licence from their home country, others require an International Driving Licence. These can be obtained from ELPA (address below) on production of a national driving licence and a passport or identification card. Again, passport size photographs will be required. A Green Card International Motor Insurance Certificate is enough for drivers from Britain and most European countries. Visitors from USA, Canada, New Zealand and Australia will be required to buy local short term insurance on entry. The minimum age for driving a car in Greece is 18.

Greek law states that a car must also carry: a fire extinguisher, first aid kit and a warning triangle but these are not always found in hired vehicles.

The carrying of fuel in cans is forbidden as is the use of main beam headlights in towns and cities. Safety belts must be worn at all times and do not be dissuaded from this by the fact that many Greek motorists do not use them. There are days when the police crack down hard on offenders. These occasions are usually well advertised but the news may escape you, especially if you are on the move. The same warning applies to motorcyclists. It is mandatory for driver and passenger to wear a crash helmet.

Information on all aspects of motoring can be obtained from the Automobile Association & Touring Club of Greece, ELPA, Athens Tower, 2-4, Messogion Street, 15 27 Athens ☎ 7791 615 to 629 & 7797 402 to 405.

### Car Hire

Rhodes is expensive for car hire and a better deal can be arranged by booking and paying in advance of departure. The minimum age for car hire is 21 but 25 for jeeps and minibuses. Clear with the hire company usage on ferries and trips out of Greece.

International car hire companies, such as Avis, Hertz, Europe Car, Budget and Eurodollar are well represented on Rhodes. In Britain, companies like Holiday Autos and Transhire (☎ 071 978 1922 & Fax 071 978 1797) offer rates including full insurance and unlimited mileage which are significantly lower than those available on the island with Transhire having the competitive edge. Both use the Holiday Autos office either at the airport or in Rhodes Town but if your holiday destination lies any distance outside, like Lindos for example, and delivery is preferred then a charge is added locally. There are also many local companies but choose carefully and examine the rates most carefully. Normally, the advertised basic rate is limited to 62 miles (100km) and does not include CDW insurance. On top of all this is VAT at 18 per cent.

Third party insurance is compulsory under Greek law and this cost will be added to the hire charge. An additional optional insurance is collision damage waiver (CDW) and it is imperative to take it. This cannot be stressed too strongly. Should you be unfortunate enough to be involved in an accident without CDW insurance and the costs cannot be recovered from a third party then the consequences can be frightening. At best you may be faced with a huge repair bill, at worst you could end up in jail until it is fully paid.

Tyres and damage to the underside of the car are mostly excluded from the insurance cover. All the unsurfaced tracks used in this book were satisfactory for hire cars at the time. However winter storms can lead to rapid deterioration and drivers must be prepared to turn back or find alternative routes should this be the case. Take time when you are accepting the car to inspect the tyres and, if not fully satisfied, do not accept the vehicle. It is worth a moment too to check that lights and indicators are fully operational. Before you drive away, make sure you have the agents telephone number.

Check with hire company if car is to be taken on ferries. Your car insurance does not cover you for damage incurred whilst on board ship.

**Motor-Cycles**
Above comments on insurance apply also to hiring a motorcycle or moped. There is a problem over crash helmets too. The law says very clearly that these must be worn but the chances that you will be able to hire them along with the bike are slim to nil. It is an unhappy situation which only compounds the personal dangers to motorcyclists in a country which has a very high accident rate. If you intend to hire a motorcycle, it is worth checking the fine print in the medical section of the holiday insurance taken out in your home country. Such is the concern over motorcycle accidents that some companies are specifically excluding injuries arising this way.

**Road Signs**
Fortunately, international road signs are used throughout the island but there may be occasions when you encounter temporary signs written in Greek. Here are a few examples:

| | |
|---|---|
| ΑΛΤ | Stop |
| ΕΛΑΤΤΩΣΑΤΕ ΤΑΧΥΤΗΤΑΝ | Reduce Speed |
| ΕΡΓΑ ΕΠΙ ΤΗΣ ΟΔΟΥ | Road Works In Progress |
| ΑΝΩΜΑΑΙΑ ΟΔΟΣΤΡΩΜΑΤΟΣ | Bad Road Surface |
| ΑΠΑΓΟΡΕΥΕΤΑΙ ΤΟ ΠΡΟΣΠΕΡΑΣΜΑ | No Overtaking |
| ΤΕΛΟΣ ΑΠΗΓΟΡΕΥΜΕΝΗΣ ΖΩΝΗΣ | End Of No-Overtaking |
| ΠΑΡΑΚΑΜΠΤΗΡΙΟΣ | Diversion |
| ΜΟΝΟΔΡΟΜΟΣ | One-Way Traffic |
| ΠΟΡΕΙΑ ΥΠΟΧΡΕΩΤΙΚΗ ΔΕΞΙΑ | Keep Right |
| ΑΠΑΓΟΡΕΥΕΤΑΙ Η ΣΤΑΘΜΕΥΣΙΣ | No Parking |
| ΑΔΙΕΞ ΟΔΟΣ | No Through Road |

**Accidents and Legal Advice**
In the event of an accident involving personal injury or damage to property, both the law and your insurance require that it is reported to the police. Start by contacting the tourist police by dialling (0241) 27423 and ask their advice. The police can also be contacted in Ialyssos 92210 and Afandou 51222.

ELPA offer free legal advice concerning Greek legislation on car accidents and insurance.

**Breakdowns**
It is a legal requirement to place a warning triangle 100m behind the car. Next step is to contact the car hire agency or if the car is private, contact Elpa by dialling 104. Elpa has reciprocal arrangements with European motoring organisations, like the British AA.

# Travelling from Rhodes

**By Boat**
Rhodes is well connected by ferry to both Athens via the port of Piraeus and to other islands including Astypalea, Crete (Heraklion, Sitia and Ag Nikoloaos), Folegandros, Halki, Kalymnos, Karpathos, Kassos, Kastelorizo, Kos, Leros, Lipsi, Milos, Nissiros Paros, Patmos, Santorini, Sifnos, Symi, Syros, Tilos.

In addition to the ferries, there are now good hydrofoil services offering shorter journey times to many of the Dodecanese islands. Services start to operate in May and provide a full programme by June. Islands served include Halki, Symi, Tilos, Kos. Onward services from Kos link up with Kalymnos, Leros, Patmos, Agathonissi, Samos, Chios, Mitilini and to Alexandroupolis and Kavala on the mainland.

**Excursion Boats**
There are daily excursion boats running to Symi and to Turkey (Marmaris) from Rhodes Town. Hydrofoils also operate excursions to Turkey. There is also a daily boat to Halki but only from Kamiros Skala.

**By Plane**
Olympic Airways operate some inter-island services from Rhodes to Crete (Heraklion), Karpathos, Kassos, Kastelorizo, Kos, Mikonos and Santorini.

# Useful and Emergency Telephone Numbers

**Rhodes Town Code 0241**

Greek National Tourist ☎ 23255 & 23655
Tourist Police ☎ 27423
Road assistance (ELPA) ☎ 104
Airport ☎ 92981/6
Rhodes General Hospital ☎ 22222
Port Authority ☎ 28888

# INDEX

MPC *Visitor's Guides* bring important practical details to your fingertips. Most of them are based upon itineraries, recognising that you may wish to tour around and take in the major places of interest.

Our unique system of symbols readily identify particular features in the text and on the maps. Each chapter finishes with lists of addresses and phone numbers we think may be of help to you. Additionally our Fact File highlights the essential information you need to know about accommodation, currency and credit cards, travel etc.

Our production team works hard to produce user-friendly guides with you in mind. We hope this helps to make your visit more rewarding.

## Visitor's Guides are produced in three categories:

Country Traveller covering particular countries and printed in full colour in a larger format.

Regional Traveller Printed in a handy pocket size and in full colour. These books cover particular areas or states within a country.

Holiday Islands Detailed information on far away islands where dreams are made! They are in the same format as the *Regional Traveller* and ideal for packing in your travel bags.

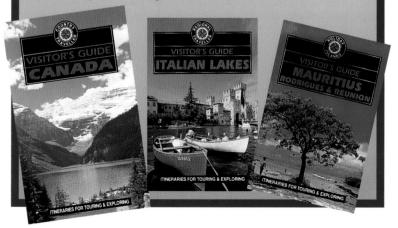

# Visitor's Guides

*Itinerary based guides for independent travellers*

**MPC**

Alps & Jura
American South West
Athens &
    Peloponnese
Austria
Austria: Tyrol &
    Vorarlberg
Bavaria
Belgium &
    Luxembourg
Black Forest
Brittany
Burgundy &
    Beaujolais
California
Canada
Champagne &
    Alsace-Lorraine
Cornwall & Isles of
    Scilly
Corsica
Costa Brava
    & Costa Blanca
Cotswolds
Crete
Cyprus
Czechoslovakia
Delhi, Agra & Rajasthan
Denmark
Devon
Dordogne
East Anglia
Egypt
Florence & Tuscany

Florida
France
Goa
Gran Canaria
Greece (mainland)
Guernsey,
    Alderney & Sark
Hampshire & Isle of
    Wight
Holland
Hungary
Iceland & Greenland
Ireland
Italian Lakes
Jersey
Kent
Lake District
Loire
Madeira
Mallorca, Menorca,
    Ibiza &
    Formentera
Malta & Gozo
Massif Central
Mauritius, Rodrigues
    & Reunion
Normandy
Normandy Landing
    Beaches
Northern Germany
Northern & Central
    Spain
Northern Ireland
Northern Italy

North Wales &
    Snowdonia
North York Moors,
    York & Coast
Northumbria
Norway
Orlando & Central
    Florida
Peak District
Peru
Portugal
Provence & Côte
    d'Azur
Rhine & Mosel
Rhodes
Sardinia
Scotland
Scotland: Lowlands
Seychelles
Somerset, Dorset &
    Wiltshire
South Africa
Southern Germany
Southern Italy
Southern Spain
    & Costa del Sol
Sweden
Switzerland
Tenerife
Treasure Houses of
    England
Turkey
USA
Yorkshire Dales &
    North Pennines